To a good friend

Whenever you find yourself I hope
this helps you catch better and bigger fish.

Naam.

Fly Fishing
with A. K.

A. K. Best

Fly Fishing
with A. K.

STACKPOLE
BOOKS

Published by
STACKPOLE BOOKS
5067 Ritter Road
Mechanicsburg, PA 17055
www.stackpolebooks.com

Printed in China

First edition

10 9 8 7 6 5 4 3 2

Illustrations by Dave Hall
Photos by John Gierach

Cover photo by John Gierach
Cover design by Wendy A. Reynolds

Library of Congress Cataloging-in-Publication Data

Best, A. K., 1933–
  Fly fishing with A.K. / A.K. Best.
     p. cm.
  Includes index.
  ISBN 0-8117-0134-4 (hardcover)
  1. Fly fishing. I. Title.

SH456.B439 2005
799.12'4—dc22

                                 2004025458

ISBN 978-0-8117-0134-1

A Toast

Here's to saints and sinners who've ever cast a dry upon the moving water and couldn't answer why.

Dedication

To Koke Winter, who taught me most of what I know about fly fishing. I learned the rest by accident.

Contents

Preface

Dave Hughes and I were sitting around a table at an authors' reception sponsored by Nick Lyons at the September 2002 Fly Tackle Dealer Show in Denver. The room was filled with authors, publishers, editors, and some other ne'er-do-wells who were standing in small groups discussing fly fishing, fly tying, rods, reels, lines, leaders, the drought, stream flows, hatches, big fish, little fish, and anything you could imagine that might be remotely connected with fly fishing. There was even a heated discussion about politics going on in one corner.

Dave asked what I was currently working on. I told him I had just finished writing and photographing the second edition of *Production Tying,* was about half done with writing the second edition of *Dyeing and Bleaching,* was sketching out some magazine articles, and was tying some flies.

He asked, "Why don't you write a book about what you haven't written?" I said, "I don't know anything else."

"Yes, you do."

"Hell I do."

"You still fish don't you?"

"Of course."

"Well, write about it."

It's a scary thought. Many very fine fly-fishing experts have written excellent books on how to fly-fish, and I told him so. How did he think the readership would be interested in yet another book that essentially dealt with how to fly-fish? "They'll be interested in how you do it," he said, "because you have some different things to say in a new voice."

I have always thought that going fly fishing simply meant that you drove to the stream, strung up your rod, tied on a fly, looked for a rising trout, and then cast to it until you caught it. It does work out that way sometimes, and it's a lot of fun. But other times it gets a little more complicated, and that's even more fun.

Dave's challenge has haunted me every waking hour (and some sleeping hours) since. So with all due respect and great admiration to those who have written a book like this before, here goes. This is what I do in an attempt to prevent complications before they arise and how I deal with them when they do.

1

Wearable Gear

How deep are your pockets? That will determine to a great extent how much of the following stuff you think you need. What you and others think you need could be an entirely different matter than what you actually need. What you actually need is equipment that will outfit you to fish in your waters. What I actually need is fewer rods and reels because I do most of my fly fishing with an 8-foot, 6-inch bamboo rod for a 5-weight line. But a feller ought to have a backup rod, right? And that thought is always the first step toward what many would label being a collector (I prefer the term "tackle junkie"). Then you begin thinking, "What if I get the chance to fish in (fill in the state/country and stream name)? I'd better get a rod for it." (And a backup.) It's a slippery slope. The next thing you know, you do get a chance to fish in (fill in the state/country and stream name), and you're damn glad you bought the tackle ahead of time. You've just convinced yourself that you'd better be prepared for anything! Next, you begin thinking about other places to go, and you outfit yourself for them (with backups). Congratulations, you've just become a tackle junkie.

It doesn't matter if you're a first-year fly fisherman or a veteran with thirty years of fly-fishing experience. You still need some basic equipment that is specifically matched to the kind of fishing you will be doing most of the time. And, as you begin collecting (when your better half is around, you should use the word *selecting;* it doesn't sound quite so extravagant) your equipment, you should always keep in mind that you *will* be fishing other waters someday.

I remember how excited I was when I outfitted myself with my first round of fly-fishing gear. I was about twenty-five years old. The rod was a solid fiberglass rod about seven feet long that I found in an Army surplus store, and the reel was an old casting reel that my dad gave me when I was about six years old. The level wind mechanism was long gone, and I thought it might hold most of a C-level line. I bought a package of those little barbed eyelets that you stick into the end of the fly line, a spool of ten-pound test monofilament for leader, and two plastic bass bugs that vaguely resembled frogs. I scrounged a spare pair of fingernail clippers to trim the knots and stuck the extra bass bug in my straw hat. I lived in Iowa at the time and waded wet in farm ponds and small warm lakes. It was a humble beginning to what my life has become. The interesting thing is I had just as much fun then as I do now. I had only the equipment that I actually needed.

I didn't know it then, but my equipment was perfectly matched to the fishing. The solid glass fly rod cast the C-level line well enough to carry the plastic frog where I was looking, and the rod had enough backbone to handle bass up to three or four pounds. I didn't know about fly reels at the time, I just wanted someplace to store the line I wasn't using.

Things are a bit different forty years later. I now own enough fly rods (with backups) and reels to fly-fish for nearly any species of fish anywhere on the planet. But each selection was made with a specific use in mind. And I've developed a genuine love of fishing for trout with bamboo rods whenever it's appropriate. I'll get into that a little later.

This chapter covers the equipment that you wear, which sometimes can be almost as important as rod, reel, line, leader, and fly. Going fishing is an exercise in survival. If you aren't properly equipped with the stuff you wear, you can easily find yourself in a miserable, even life-threatening situation. Fly fishing is an activity that should be enjoyed without any worry of personal welfare or comfort. With a little forethought and some minor expenditures, it's a simple matter to eliminate any concern of this sort. Plan well and choose wisely, and you'll be ready for any complication that may arise when you're on the water.

I'm going to begin the equipment discussion with some thoughts on waders. My first pair of waders was the rubber-soled, cleat-foot, canvas-upper type that was so popular back in the 50s. They just looked right to me, and that's all that was available. I forgot what they cost, but I do remember that when I finally trashed them, they had something like forty-three patches! I busted them the day I put them on and one of the boots separated from the leg! I've owned just about every kind of chest-high wader made since then, including hip boots. Maybe it's my age, or maybe it's just the experience of having fly-fished for over forty years, but I really don't see the need for a pair of waders that comes up to my armpits. All they do is allow me to wade in way too deep. In fact, if you're in up to your armpits, you're likely going to have trouble wading back out and you're already standing where you should be fishing. I often hear someone say, "Well, I need to get in that deep to reach the other side." So I ask, "Are all the trout on the other side?" There's never an answer.

I think the answer to the wader question is a pair of waist-high waders. With waist-highs, you can get your hand in the pocket of your jeans to find your car keys, your upper body is not encased in a rubber suit that will make you sweat all day, and they will keep you from wading into trouble. I have discovered that it's a lot easier to wade into trouble than it is to wade out of it. I've fished a lot of streams throughout the United States and can't think of a reason that I'd ever need anything more than a pair of waist-high waders. I figure if the water is too deep for waist-high waders, I should be in a boat!

If you think you can't live if you don't have a pair of armpit-high waders, by all means wear a tight wading belt any time you're in the water, no mater how shallow it may be. It's amazing how fast a pair of waders can fill with water when you fall down, and someday you *will* fall down. Many wader manufacturers include the belt as an integral part of the wader. If you don't have a belt on your waders, find a nylon belt with a quick-release buckle. Believe me, that's important when nature makes an urgent call on your bladder! All the waist-high waders I've seen come with belts, but they never seem to be the correct height. I bought a pair of heavy-duty suspenders and leave them attached. The suspenders will keep your waist-highs at a comfortable height and prevent the wrinkles at your knees from wearing through and causing leaks that are almost impossible to mend.

I've tried hip boots and always get a wet crotch. They're nice in the summer when it really gets hot, but then so are Gore-Tex waist-highs. It seems that I too often find myself in a spot where I could wade around a boulder or log if I could only wade in just higher than my crotch. The other choice is to climb out of the stream and walk around a boulder field, slog through a swamp, or climb over a logjam and risk ripping a hole in a spot that will always be knee high. I've been wearing a pair of waist-high Gore-Tex waders for the past five years and have not been sorry. I can still stand in water deep enough that I should be fishing, it's easy to climb in and out of a float boat, I can usually find a place to cross the stream if I feel I really need to be on the other side, and I think they've saved my life a few times by keeping me from wading into trouble. By the way, if you are going to teach your young son or daughter how to fly-fish, for heaven's sake *do not* get him or her a pair of waders! Until they are five feet tall and weigh more than 120 pounds, kids simply don't have enough body mass (or, more importantly, experience) to wade in water up to their armpits. And for heaven's sake don't make them wade wet; they'll be miserably cold in no time. Get them a pair of hippers. You'll both be glad you did.

Felt-soled boots (the kind you put on over your stocking-foot waders) are a must if you fish anyplace where there are rocks in the stream. They provide much-needed ankle support, and they'll save you from stumbling around after a slip on a greasy rock and spooking every trout within twenty yards both up- and downstream. Slipping on a rock with rubber cleat-soled boots is much like doing a sloppy (often wet) river dance. There is also the felt-soled ballet, performed when the rocks are covered with algae slime. The footwear I find ideal is tungsten-studded felt-soled boots. But you have to be careful on dry rocks, and you won't be able to get in a float boat with them on. Those little tungsten spikes will scratch the hell out of the bottom of an expensive float boat, and you won't be able to stand up in it without sliding all over. The guide will either make you take them off or you won't be able to go on the float trip of a lifetime. If you are a serious fly fisher, you'll probably end up with two pairs of felt-soled boots, one studded and one not.

I wear thick wool socks inside the neoprene stocking feet of my breathable waders, whether it's summer or winter. Don't make the mistake I did by trying to wear another pair of socks under the wool socks for wintertime fishing. The extra layer that I thought would keep my toes warm a little longer actually made my boots fit a little too tight and cut off blood supply to my toes, and they got cold sooner! The best thing to do when your toes begin to get cold is to get out of the stream and walk around for a few minutes.

A thin pair of fleece long johns is all you need for winter fishing under the breathables. I don't advise Levis or any other type of cotton pants, since there is virtually no insulating value to them and they do not wick moisture from your skin. Summertime is fun time; I wear a pair of wool socks and my Jockey shorts under the breathable waders. The waders breathe and my skin stays dry. I would strongly advise wearing fleece for warmth under your rain shell when the temperature begins to dip. I have a heavy fleece vest and lightweight and heavyweight fleece jackets. By layering combinations of these fleece garments under my rain shell, I can stay comfortable in all but the cruelest conditions. Fleece is very light to carry and doesn't weigh heavily on my body, and I believe the layers of fleece trap more air than any thick wool sweater I own.

I hardly ever go fishing without my wading staff, no matter how small or large the stream. It doubles as a fine walking stick when I'm hiking in and a third balance point when I'm sloshing around in a little boulder-strewn stream. And it's a wonderful testing device when you're wading in murky water and can't see the bottom two feet down, or fishing in a pond that has a mucky bottom. It's saved me from drowning or getting wet hundreds of times, especially when I've been standing in thigh-deep ice-cold water and decide it's time to turn around and head back to shore. Wading staff or not, you should always turn your body into the current as you turn around. It's a lot easier to lean forward into the force of the current than it is to lean backward. The sudden force of the water against your back will probably put you face down in the stream. Use the wading staff to help keep your balance, and don't try to hurry. I think my feelings about using a wading staff are tempered to a degree by my aging body, coupled with the desire to stay alive so I can fish another day.

Ah, the fly vest. I keep mine hanging on a hook where it's the first thing I see every morning when I go downstairs to my office/fly-tying room. I look at it to remind myself of what I really should be doing!

Each time I put it on, heavy as it is, I remember past fishing excursions, the streams I've been on, and friends I've fished with while wearing it. There's a dark greasy stain left from the day I was frantically changing flies high on the St. Vrain and forgot to close the top on my bottle of Gink. The lower left outside pocket is smeared with blood stains (mine), from the day I damn near broke my left arm while sliding down a gravel slope and grasping for any branch in reach. One of the pockets is sticky with dust from a bottle of fine desiccant that burst its cap. In the big pocket way in the back of my vest are a couple of highly flexible honey and oats granola bars and a badly misshapen Snickers bar. I have no idea how long they've been there, but I'll leave them there, just in case.

My vest is loaded with "just in case" items. That's probably why it seems to weigh so much. Actually, even with a wood frame landing net, it's only a couple of ounces over six pounds. There are those who frown on the use of a net, but it's how I learned to land and release fish quickly. I seem to fumble around a lot longer without one.

One of reasons why my granola bars are so badly crumbled is because I carry Band-Aids and a little bottle of Mercurochrome in a small tin box. In another small tin box is a little tube of Barge cement for plugging tiny holes that appear now and then in my waders. Each time I take a rest and lean against a tree or boulder, I pulverize the granola bars a little more when they get between the tins and my backrest. I've only had to make use of the items in the two tins once in the last six or seven years and was damn glad I had their contents with me. I used the Barge cement to repair a small hole in the left knee of my waders on the same day the Band-Aids and Mercurochrome fixed a puncture wound in my left hand when I grabbed a branch full of broken stubs on my slide down the gravelly slope. If this should ever happen to you, fix the hole in your waders first! Your hand will bleed out nicely while you patch your waders, and by the time you get your hand fixed, the Barge cement will be almost dry enough to resume fishing!

The big back pocket also contains an old Kodak aluminum film can full of small wooden matches and a piece of the striker from the side of the matchbox. I've only used it a couple of times and was thankful to have dry matches on a cold, rainy day when the flint on my lighter gave up. I keep the film can in a Ziploc bag with a few inch-wide strips of white birch bark with which I can start a fire in all but the worst of downpours.

Speaking of white strips, there is another Ziploc bag in the big back pocket that contains twelve feet of toilet paper, some to use and some to spare. (You never know!) I also keep a couple of long boot laces back there, just in case I should ever need them for something, like tying a couple of branches together to make a quick frame for a shelter if I have to spend the night in the mountains. The back pocket of my vest is essentially a grab bag of stuff that is integral to a day's fishing, such as two pieces of bike inner tube for use as rod pullers (to help pull apart the ferrules after a day of fishing), a pair of sun gloves, a pair of neoprene gloves for those days at 10,000 feet when it suddenly turns cold, a quart canteen full of water, a couple of extra rolls of film, and a rolled-up rain shell that is more often used as a windbreaker.

Hanging on the front of my vest is a safety pin that I fastened to the zipper tab with a looped ball chain. It's a good aid in picking out those little triple figure 8 knots in my tippet as well as poking the head cement from some of my hastily tied flies. Also hanging in front is a pair of expensive, fine-point fly-tying scissors on a heavy-duty zinger. I don't like those little clips for nipping off leader tags, because that's all they're good for. I can trim leader tags and the bottom of a hackle collar with the scissors. The scissors will function for any number of other clipping chores, and their fine points are much easier to use than the blunt ends of a pair of clippers. You can use the scissors to cut away those damned snap-together cloth tabs that I guess we're supposed to use to hold the front of the vest together. There's already a zipper for that, and all the tabs do is grab your fly line just when you want to shoot an extra twelve feet to the trout of a lifetime. Another item that hangs from a small zinger, but is stored in a small inside pocket, is a leader gauge. I tie my own leaders and want to be certain of the exact diameters each time I repair my leader or add tippet.

Since I mentioned leaders, I carry all the spools of leader material I'll need to completely rebuild a leader from the first butt section to 7X tippet. I learned long ago that if I used knotless tapered leaders I was using another person's idea of how I should cast and under what conditions every day. I can adjust any portion of my leader at any time to suit any fishing condition. I've had to do this many times, and I consider the leader kit I carry on two heavy ball chains in the extra reel spool pockets of my vest to be essential. Three more essential items are a small bottle of sunscreen in one small pocket, a small bottle of liquid bug repellent in another, and my fishing license.

When I lived in Michigan I always carried a good compass because one can get lost in the thick north woods in less than five minutes. All you have to do is decide to take a shortcut back to the truck. You can be ten feet from a road and not know it because the woods are often so dense you can't see more than six or eight feet ahead. Carrying a compass in the Rockies where I live now is almost useless because there are so many ore deposits and deeply buried meteors. Shortcutting back to the truck is a matter of following the stream through deep canyons.

The pockets for my fly boxes are usually the fullest. I'm one of those types who always carries enough flies to open a small streamside shop.

But I do try to sort the flies by season to limit my selections. There is always a possibility of a midge hatch, so I bring the midge box. Since blue-winged olives can be found hatching nearly any time of year, I keep a box full of duns, parachutes, and spinners for the BWOs. The third box is full of nymphs, with everything from size 22 midge larvae to a couple of size 6 stonefly nymphs. A fourth fly box I always bring along is a small box of a dozen or more "never fail" streamers.

Come spring, I add dry-fly boxes that are full of Red Quills, Adamses, Royal Wulffs, ants, beetles, and caddisflies. As summer comes on, I stick in a box of hoppers and large drakes. When fall blends into winter, I begin paring the selections back to the basic four.

I hate it when the old vest finally wears out. The zippers don't work, all the Velcro has become useless, and the worn-out stitching that I have meticulously replaced with needle and thread has deteriorated to the point that I'm afraid one of the pockets will fall off. It seems that just when I become so familiar with my vest that I can find anything in it in pitch black darkness, it's time to get a new one. And of course that kind of vest is no longer being made. It's frustrating. It'll take at least two years to get acquainted with a new vest because all the fly box pockets will be different sizes and in new places. And many of the fly shops carry only a limited selection of vests. None of them seems to have enough pockets.

My favorite kind of fishing hat is a soft cotton hat with a wide brim all around it. It protects my ears and much of my face and neck from the scorching sun. I can pull the front down low over my eyes to block out the low angle of the sun, which can be blinding during early morning and late evening hours. It fits comfortably under the hood of my raincoat, and it soaks up bug repellent very nicely, which, by the way, does help to keep some of the black flies and mosquitoes at a distance and gives the hat a nice, well-used look. On those really hot days, I can dip my hat in the stream and the wet hat keeps my head cool for a while. Although I hate doing it, I do toss the hat in the washing machine (about once every two years) because the sweat stains, mud smears, and fish slime that season the hat do get a bit offensive. If you decide to go with a cotton hat, be very careful about its size. You want it snug enough that the wind can't blow it off, but slightly big to allow for shrinking after washing. You can prevent shrinking appreciably by taking the hat out of the dryer while it's still a little damp and wearing it until it's completely dry. If you don't do this, it'll shrink at least a full size.

You can find long-sleeve shirts with large pockets in most fly shops or catalogs. They are designed for the active sportsman and function quite well. However, I caution you to avoid those with Velcro tabs on the pockets. You will eventually lose whatever you have put in them when you bend over to net or release a fish. I speak from experience when I say I cannot trust Velcro to hold any pocket together for more than two minutes. There are one or two manufacturers that make shirts with buttons large enough to secure ample pocket flaps. When your fingers are cold, you can handle large buttons more efficiently than those little baby pea-size buttons that are used on dress shirts. Long sleeves will protect your arms and wrists from damaging sunburn as well as provide you some degree of warmth when the temperature begins to fall. Some shirts are constructed with ventilating panels in the back and sides. Wearing a fly vest pretty much negates that function. Be sure to choose a shirt in some shade of green, tan, or brown; you'll blend in with your surroundings much better. Trout can see a white or bright yellow shirt long before you get close enough to make a cast.

I'd also suggest you consider a pair of sun gloves. Thirty or forty years of sunburned hands can cause skin problems. Skin cancer is a complication no one needs, and it'll probably keep you off the trout stream.

A raincoat that will roll up into a small package and fit in the back pocket of your vest is a must. Once again, size is very important. You'll have to decide how you want to use the raincoat—under or over your loaded vest. My advice is to get one that is large enough to easily zip when you wear it over your vest. A heavy vest gets even heavier when it's soaking wet. I found an XX-large Helly Hansen rain jacket a couple of years ago and it's the best one I've ever used. I carry it with me at all times because I've learned that the people who have jobs telling you what the weather is going to be are usually reporting what's happening at the moment and not what will happen later. A good rain jacket also makes a wonderful windbreaker that will help keep you warm a little longer. Make sure it has at least one pocket with a zipper and two side pockets for cold hands.

The reasons for using Polaroid glasses are well known and much discussed. My advice here is that if you wear prescription glasses, by all means get a pair of prescription Polaroids. I've tried those clip-on types, and the space between my glasses and the clip-ons causes a disturbing reflection. There are two kinds: one that clips to the rim of your glasses, and another that flips up when you don't need them. The flip-up model will scratch the lenses of your prescription glasses where the little clips slide on, and the version that clips to the frame of your regular glasses is a pain to put on. I've had a couple of pair go springing out into the stream because I didn't get them quite right. Bite the bullet and go see your optometrist and get a pair of prescription Polaroids with hardened plastic lenses that also have UV protection (bifocals if you need them). They're not cheap, but then neither was your rod and reel, both of which are worthless if you can't see the fish or the fly.

If you are a fly tier, you'd be very wise to spend a little money and purchase a good 35mm single-lens reflex camera with a 50mm macro lens so you can get some great close-up photos of the insects in your favorite stream. Use slide film, and project your bug photos on a screen so you can study the proportions and subtleties of color. A good 200-speed color film will allow you to shoot photos very early in the morning and quite late in the evening. Faster films can get a little grainy, but they're getting better each year. The 50mm macro lens also functions very well for shooting flowers, close-ups of your fish, your buddy with a big (or little) fish, and ordinary snapshots of the campsite or your loaded vehicle. You can record each fishing trip for sharing with friends or reminiscing later when you're too old and decrepit to wade a stream. The camera can't lie but will preserve some wonderful memories for you.

Digital cameras are becoming popular, but they're expensive. Good ones cost twice as much or more than good film cameras. A sharp photo slide of a size 18 blue-winged olive projected on a four-by-six-foot screen becomes a bug that's nearly four feet long! There might be a way to do it, but I'm not aware of how you would do that with a digital camera and your computer. I've learned so much from the slides I have taken over the years. Photos are a great resource.

Sunscreens and bug repellents are available everywhere. Use them. Be careful of the sunscreens that are rated 40 SPF or higher. Some people (I'm one) are allergic to the high SPF. I break out in a rash that's worse than any sunburn. I can use a water-resistant SPF 15, so I just put on more throughout the day. If you have any kind of skin problem that's sun-related, you should visit a dermatologist for some guidance on what to use. I offer the same advice for bug repellents.

Day after day of long hours on the stream, lake, or ocean can do a number on your hands. Your hands can get dry and cracked from becoming wet and dry hundreds of times during the week. The best prevention

I have found for this is to apply a few drops of a 50/50 mixture of glycerin and water to your hands just before you go to bed each night. Massage it into both hands just as you would any other lotion. You can get a small bottle of glycerin from most well-stocked pharmacies. Mix it half and half with water and put it in your overnight bag. It's a good hint for fly tiers who live in dry climates as well. It's a good inexpensive and effective hand lotion.

Here are a few words on fly floatants. They really aren't floatants at all but rather waterproofing agents. There are a bunch of products on the market these days that are supposed to make your dry fly float. Well, if your fly is constructed of material that is lighter than water, it will float. What makes a fly sink is when it begins to soak up water or gets slimed by a fish. Waterproofing the fly will prevent it from soaking up water as you fish it. You cannot prevent your fly from getting slimed after you land a fish. However, I have noticed that if I don't net the fish, but slide my line-hand thumb and forefinger down the tippet and slide the hook out while the fish is still in the water, there is virtually no slime deposited on the fly. There are some products on the market that are advertised to remedy the problem of the slimed fly. Don't use them! One is a patch that you're supposed to squeeze your fly in after landing a fish. The patch does soak up some of the slime, but you are also squeezing slime into your fly as you do this. Your fly will sink after doing this. Then there is the stuff that a few of us call "fairy dust." It's a fine, white-powdered desiccant that is supposed to absorb all the moisture in a couple of seconds. What it actually does is dehydrate the fish slime, which will rehydrate as soon as your fly touches the water. In addition, you're left with a fine powdery residue on your fly even after you try to blow the excess off. What does this residue do? What it is supposed to do, soak up water!

I don't often endorse any product, but I just haven't found anything that works as well as Gerke's Gink when it comes to waterproofing a fly. Always apply Gink to your dry fly to waterproof it before making the first cast. When I apply Gink to the fly I make sure it's in a semiliquid state. Then I squeeze a drop on my left index finger, place the fly directly on top of the drop of Gink, and then press the liquid into the fly with my left thumb pad with the intention of impregnating the fly right down to the hook shank.

So what do I do when a fly gets slimed? False-cast it three or four times in such a way that the fly slaps the water much like a sloppy backcast. The action dislodges all the fish slime, and the fly will float just as

well as it did when you made your first cast. Of course you should execute this in a spot that is far away from your next presentation. If you
follow these hints, you can fish the same fly all day, catch a dozen or more
fish, and never have to reapply the Gink. And if that is not enough of a
good thing, I have some flies in my dry-fly box that I ginked a year ago,
and when I tie one on to the tippet, it floats just as well as it did last year.

2

Tackle

RODS

Short rods, long rods, medium rods, fast rods, slow rods, spey rods, 0- to 15-weight rods, graphite rods, titanium rods, fiberglass rods, bamboo rods; the possibilities are nearly endless and can be very confusing to a newcomer to the sport, let alone someone who has fly-fished for years.

The quality and number of rods available today were unimaginable thirty years ago. The technology of rod building has developed to a point that you have to look hard to find a poor casting tool. Although there is a perceived value to an expensive rod and how well it will cast, I've cast some $600 rods that didn't cast two cents better than some $150 rods. Each fly fisher has his own preferences as to how a rod should cast and feel while casting. That's why there are so many different brands and models. It's the same with automobiles. If one manufacturer made cars that were better than all the rest, there wouldn't be others. I drive a Ford, you drive a Chevy; we both like the vehicle we have because it suits our needs.

There is a wide variety of tapers and actions that can be built into a rod, no matter what it's made of. You need to cast as many makes and models as you can before you make a selection. Always keep in mind how you intend to use the rod. For example, I looked for almost three years for a 9-foot 8-weight 4-piece graphite rod that I could use for both striper fishing in the ocean and huge brook trout on large fast rivers in Labrador. I wanted a rod that could cast a WF 9 multi-tip line to the horizon and could handle both the super-fast sinking heads as well as it did the floating head. I'd about given up on ever finding such a tool until one day at a fly-fishing show in Somerset, New Jersey, a friend said, "Here, you gotta try this rod." I did and bought it on the spot. It was less than $200. I purchased a multi-tip WF 9 line and put it and three hundred yards of backing on a big wide-arbor reel. I cut off about the last twenty feet of the running line from the multi-tip line, which allowed me to put an extra one hundred yards of backing on the reel spool. One large striper took me into the last one hundred yards of backing a couple of years ago. I was damn glad I made the adjustment *before* I used it. This rod is the perfect tool for my needs.

I have an old 8-foot 3-piece Granger bamboo rod that will throw a WF 7 floating line ninety feet with little effort, but 6- to 9-pound brook trout in heavy water in Labrador are too much for it. That kind of application amounts to rod abuse. I own another 8-foot 3-piece Granger for a 5-weight line that is rather slow and delicate. I wouldn't think of using it on the Frying Pan River in Colorado, where rainbows and browns can weigh in at 3 to 6 pounds. At the same time, I have a Mike Clark 8½-foot bamboo rod for a 5-weight line that will stop a 24-inch rainbow in white water, yet is delicate enough to cast fifteen feet of leader and a size 22 BWO tied to 36 inches of 7X tippet as fast or slow as I please.

The lightest line weight rod I own is a 7½-foot bamboo for a 4-weight line. I use it occasionally, when I'm fishing a small stream with trout no larger than 8 to 14 inches on a day with no wind. If there are larger trout, I'm stressing both the trout and the rod. The first fish I landed on that rod weighed 8½ pounds in a wet net. I figure it was an honest 7½-pound fish. I played the fish off the butt section and led it to a sandy beach. I'll never use it like that again. But it was a hell of a baptism for a new rod!

I'm confused by the letter/number designations some rod makers use to identify their graphite rods. Maybe the codes mean something to the maker, but they don't tell me much. If you are going to try testing some rods, you'll need to take notes to document what should be written on the rod in the first place. What ever happened to "9' DT6F, medium fast?" And maybe including the year the rod was made. Instead, we see something like XSDUPR3-44Y (and the company name, of course). It's a little like trying to figure out who made the fancy automobile idling next to you at a stoplight. Remember Plymouth Deluxe and Chrysler Royal?

Nowadays the rods and cars look alike except for the list of letters and numbers on them.

When choosing a rod you need to consider your casting ability (some rods are quite user-friendly, others are not), the size of the water (stream, pond, lake, or ocean), and the species and size of the fish you are likely to catch. Generally speaking, you need progressively longer rods with increasingly heavier lines for larger water and heavier species.

Remember that everyone who fly-fishes has a favorite rod and will try to convince you to get one like it. There may even be some shop owners who have rods they'd like to sell for a number of questionable motives: 1, they have more rods of a particular brand in stock than they want; 2, the price markup is good for them; or 3, there are only a few rods by a particular maker left in stock, and they'd like to unload them so they can sign up with a new manufacturer. Most shop owners are trustworthy, but be warned. You could end up with a rod that you won't like. Be wary of the person who says, "Have I got a deal for you!" That kind of deal is usually better for him than you. Do your shopping at established fly shops with good reputations, and you won't go wrong.

Some of the expensive graphite rods come with lifetime warranties, and the manufacturer will replace the rod if it gets broken for any reason. Usually the only expense to you will be postage and handling. That's an attractive deal, but, my theory is that you are paying for a couple of replacement rods up front. My preference is to find a graphite rod that costs around $200 or less and is good for my casting style. If I never break the rod, I'm several hundred dollars ahead of the game. If I do break it, I'll buy another and still be money ahead!

Try many rods before you buy. Take your time and don't make the mistake of trying to cast the entire line in a few minutes. Stand sideways to your rod and watch the backcast loop. It should look exactly like the forward cast loop. Try short distances first. Determine how much line you must have in the air before the rod begins to load up and go to work. Will the rod allow you to cast the leader and three feet of line as well as ten, twenty, or thirty feet of line? Can you cast a tight loop and an open loop; does it like to roll-cast; how much line will it easily pick up; how much line will it comfortably shoot? These are considerations you should make as you try the rod. Do most of your trial casting at the same distances you will be fishing. I always figure that when I'm fishing small to medium streams, I only need to cast twenty or thirty feet. If I must cast farther than that to reach the fish, I move upstream.

For those of you who are beginning fly fishers, sign up for a fly-casting class. Find an instructor who is a qualified, experienced fly fisher with years of time on the water. You'll learn more in a couple of three or four hour classes than you'll learn by yourself in ten years. A good instructor will be able to diagnose any casting problems you may be having and advise you on the rod you're going to need for the fishing you intend to do. Classes sometimes include some stream entomology that will be invaluable to you when you do begin to go fishing. This portion of the class usually includes tips on how to identify insects and their various stages of aquatic growth.

And by all means, purchase your tackle from a local fly shop. You'll end up going there anyway for small purchases such as leaders, flies, and floatants. You'll be treated much better if you are recognized as a loyal customer. If you need to have a guide wrap replaced, are you bold enough to take a rod you bought from an on-line site or mail-order catalog to your local dealer for repair? I wouldn't blame him if he told you to take it back where you bought it. Local fly shops offer fine service to their customers and deserve our support.

REELS

I haven't counted them, but I'll bet there are a hundred reel manufacturers. The price of a good reel can range from something equivalent to my monthly house payment to the cost of a good bottle of scotch. You can, of course, make a personal statement if you want to choose a reel that costs multiples of 100 dollars. But all reels perform the same function: a place to store the fly line you're not using and some backing. Like rods, reels come in all manner of sizes, weights, finishes, drag mechanisms, and designs. If you browse through the cases in a few fly shops and scan a few catalogs, you'll be able to select the reel you want *and need.* You can get a good reel for less than $200. By good, I mean one that will last for a decade or two, has an adjustable drag, has an exposed spool rim for palming when some fish you weren't expecting screams away with most of your backing, can easily be changed from right-hand to left-hand wind, and has a spool release that requires no tools when you want to change spools quickly.

Take care to notice how the reel handle and knob are designed and attached. If you pick a reel with a classy S curve handle with a knob on one end that is a separate unit from the spool, you may be aggravated if there is a wide enough space between the reel frame and the handle for a loose loop of line to fall into. I prefer a reel with a knob integral to the spool. The wind-up knob itself should be slightly conically shaped with the base toward the spool. This shape will allow a loop of fly line to slide off more easily. Avoid straight cylindrical and hourglass-shaped knobs. Both will tend to reach out and grab a loose loop of fly line or, worse yet, a loop of backing at exactly the wrong time.

Carefully examine how the reel foot is attached to the reel frame. This may not be such a big deal for the average freshwater fly fisher, but it is for those who go after huge saltwater fish, big steelhead, or salmon. Once while steelhead fishing in Michigan, I saw a reel fall from its foot (which was still firmly attached to the rod). It didn't come apart because the screws fell out, it broke! Further examination showed an old hairline crack that probably happened when the reel was dropped sometime earlier. So there was the fly fisher, trying frantically to land his steelhead and a fly reel, both of which were headed downstream! Any reel foot that appears flimsily attached to the reel frame will surely fail on the largest fish you have ever hooked. If there are any screws holding the reel foot to the reel frame (or any other screws on your reel), take them out (one at a time), apply a tiny drop of Barge cement or Pliobond, and firmly screw them back in. They won't be able to work themselves loose, but you'll be able to remove them if you need to. Be sure to use the correct size screwdriver when you attempt this.

Your reel should have some kind of very smooth line guard. A line guard is an addition to the reel frame that provides a smooth surface for the fly line to run out or be reeled in and adds years to the life of the fly line by reducing friction from the reel frame.

Most reels are sold with a bag for storage and protection. An old wool sock will work if the reel you want doesn't come with a bag.

Don't get talked into buying a toy-size reel just because you have a light, 2-, 3-, or 4-weight rod. The temptation to use a light line rod where big fish live is more than some people can resist. If you are using a reel that will only hold twenty or thirty yards of backing and the fly line, I can guarantee you are going to hook into a fish someday that will take all your fly line and backing on the first or second run. You will lose the fish or all your line when the backing suddenly hits the spool arbor knot and cuts itself off. I think you should have at least one hundred yards of backing on a reel for freshwater fishing. Even then, I've had to break off a few fish because I could see the reel arbor glowing through the last ten yards of backing, a sickening feeling.

Years ago I bought a Scientific Anglers System 7 reel and six spare spools. The theory was that a light line rod doesn't have the fish-fighting power of a heavier line rod, so I would probably need more backing on the spools with lighter lines. The math goes something like this: lighter line weight = smaller line diameter = more backing capacity. So I loaded the spools as follows: WF 7 F, WF 7 S, DT 6 F, WF 6 F, DT 5 F, WF 5 F, and DT 4 F. Seven spools counting the one that came with the reel. But one day I got to thinking—what if I dropped the reel frame and it broke? It took me a year to find a spare System 7 frame, which is still in its original box. But I have it.

I have a few expensive reels that were made from solid bar stock by computer-driven machines. The spools are perfectly balanced, they are pleasing to the eye, they hold my fly lines and a couple of hundred yards of backing, and they provide the balance I like when they are attached to my rods. Most of them are a little over-engineered. With two of them, I need a small screwdriver to remove the spools. Did you ever have your leader tippet get behind the spool and get tangled around the mechanism inside? I hate it when that happens. In my haste to disassemble the reel to get my tippet dislodged, there's a good chance I'm going to lose one of those little screws that hold the frame together. I will never buy a reel that does not have a ventilated spool. Those little holes are a great place to thread the end of your tippet through to prevent it from getting behind the spool in the first place. But sometimes the tippet decides to make your life miserable by pulling itself out of the hole and hiding behind the reel spool. There's a little self-adhesive button you can stick to the side of your reel for keeping your tippet in place. I just can't bring myself to stick something that cost a dollar to the side of a reel that cost a couple of hundred.

I really like the sound of a click pawl–drag system when I hook a fish that makes a run and the reel screams. It's rather an empty feeling when you have a fish on and fighting and there is only a whisper as the line runs out through the guides. Some reel manufacturers design their drag systems to be audible or silent, and some make reels that are silent. In either case, the drag system must be adjustable. I've seen some disc-drag systems that are strong enough to stop a truck, and I've always wondered why that was needed or even advisable. A drag set that tight will allow you to lean into a fish hard enough to break your rod or the leader. When a big strong fish makes a screaming run, it is best played directly off the reel with the rod pointed straight at it and the drag set just tight enough that when the fish stops, the spool won't overrun and create a hell of a backlash. A big fish will go where it wants, and your best tactic is to allow that to happen while applying some pressure. Remember that when there is a lot of line and backing out, there is increased water friction (drag) on the fish as it tries to get away. By tightening the drag setting, you are only adding to the chances that something will break. It's a far better idea to reduce the drag setting in cases like that.

Find out if the reel you intend to buy is reversible from right-hand to left-hand wind and if you need a degree in engineering to be able to make that adjustment. Most good reels come with a little sheet of instructions on care, cleaning, and lubrication. Somewhere on this sheet will be instructions on how to reverse the wind. And if you purchased the reel from your local fly shop, you can go back and they'll be glad to make the switch for you. Consider how you're going to use the reel. If you're naturally right-handed and intend to fish for steelhead, large salmon, or any saltwater game fish, you should be sure that the reel is in a right-hand wind mode. You can wind right-handed a lot faster than you can left-handed, if you're a right-handed person. All my trout reels are set up for left-hand wind because I figure I'll have to change rod hands at precisely the wrong time when I go to net the fish with my left hand. My saltwater reels are set up for right-hand wind because of the blistering speed of most of these species. In either case, I want to get all the loose line back on the reel as soon as possible. Loose line on the deck of a boat or trailing downstream is a disaster waiting to happen.

I always load my reels with as much backing as I can and still maintain about one fourth of an inch of empty spool space after all the fly line has been wound on. The reason is that I probably won't be very careful winding the backing and line back onto the spool as I play a big fish. Incidentally, it's always a good idea to strip off the used line and backing and carefully wind it back on after landing a fish that took out all your line and some backing. Then you can make certain that it all goes back on the spool smoothly with no fallen over wraps.

Periodically remove the spool, rinse the inside of the frame with hot tap water, wipe off the post with a clean soft cloth, use a Q-Tip to clean out the cylinder that the post goes into, and relubricate both surfaces with a high-quality reel lube product. Sometimes I find I need to use an old toothbrush and a few drops of lacquer thinner to scrub all the black gunk out of a click pawl–drag system. You should apply a drop of oil to these parts as well.

FLY LINES

Recommending fly lines can be dangerous ground, so I'll tread lightly. Given the number of manufacturers of rods and reels, I'm a little surprised there aren't more makers of fly line. Not that there aren't enough as it is. I think the reason there aren't more is because those who have been doing it are so good at it. A handful of suppliers gives us hundreds of designs and dozens of colors to choose from, all of them good for the purposes they were intended. You'll eventually find some brand you favor over others, and that's good because it means that you are becoming a discerning consumer. It also means that you are developing a casting style that you're comfortable with on the waters you fish.

Beginning fly fishers are at the mercy of those giving advice. It's true with rods, reels, and especially fly lines. You have to understand that rod manufacturers sometimes recommend you use line weights that are underrated or overrated for their rods. And some are right on. Some rods are designed to cast as many as 3 or 4 line weights. These rods always cast one line weight better than the others. One rod manufacturer rates rods by the weight forward line it recommends. The thing to remember here is that the rods are designed and field-tested by other fly fishers who make rods that feel good to them. Each company has its own team of testers. Most of the time these folks are highly skilled casters and could cast a broomstick if asked. Try to stay with the top name line makers and try their lines on *your* rod. Most fly shops will have reels spooled with demo lines just for this purpose. If you have a 9-foot graphite rod that's rated for a DT 5 floating line, for example, try every brand of DT 5 F line you can get your hands on. One of them will work better for you than the rest.

I own several bamboo rods and prefer to use the old peach-colored Cortland 444 lines on them. My cane rods seem happier with that combination. I also own a few graphite rods, some of which like Scientific Anglers lines, some like Air Flow, some like Rio lines, and some like Wulff lines. I purchased some of my rods to fish small to medium streams, some for large rivers, some for lakes and ponds, and a couple for saltwater fishing. Like the rods, I chose lines that suit my needs and that seem to make the rods happy. I don't want to leave anyone who makes fly lines out of the picture here; it's just that I've tried lines until I've found one for a particular rod and its intended use and then stopped trying others. You purchased your rod and reel with specific kinds of fishing in mind. Select your fly lines with the same thought.

Before purchasing any fly line, consider where you will be fishing and how far you may have to cast. I have weight-forward lines for every trout rod I own because I never know when I'm going to get the opportunity to fish a pond or lake where longer casting distances are often required. As a general rule you can always go up one line weight for a weight-forward line. That is to say, if your rod is rated for a DT 5 F line, you will comfortably be able to cast a WF 6 F line with most rods, both graphite and bamboo. However, you must be very careful here, since some rod manufacturers rate their rods by what weight-forward line it is designed to cast. If you do a lot of lake or pond fishing, you'd be wise to get a multi-tip line that will allow you to fish dry or at nearly any depth you wish. It is possible to loop-connect a couple of sinking tips to get down quickly and deep if you have a multi-tip line. But be advised that it won't be fun to cast or pretty to watch! Such looping of heads is best done if you're fishing from a boat or personal flotation craft where you can feed the line out as you drift. These lines often come with leader sections that are also designed to either float or sink at variable rates. Combinations of different tips and leaders will allow you to fish nearly every condition you're likely to encounter.

You have two options when it comes to attaching the backing to your reel, the fly line to the backing, and then the leader to the working end of the fly line. You can have the fly shop do this for you (you really have to trust that they know what they're doing) or you can do it yourself (and you'd better know what you're doing!).

If you insist on using one of those small-size reels, you can cut a double-taper line in half and be able to get a lot more backing on the tiny spool. Save the other half of the fly line for use later, and label it so you don't forget what it is. I always attach the backing to the spool arbor with a loop of backing that I make by tying a double overhand knot to create a small loop. Remove the spool from the frame, thread the backing through the edge of the frame, pull the single strand of backing through the loop to make a larger loop, and slide the larger loop over one side of the reel spool. Put the spool back into the frame and you're ready to wind on the backing. Always make sure that the adjustable drag is set as low as it will go when you do this.

Note: if you opt to have the fly shop do the work for you, ask them if they use a line winder for spooling reels. Most of them do. Then ask them to please remove the spool from the reel frame before they begin. I once watched a young shop clerk clamp a reel in a line winder, attach the backing with a slip knot, and proceed to wind a couple of hundred yards of backing onto the spool (with the spool in the frame and the adjustable drag on). I had to leave. I was in the same shop a couple of weeks later when the guy with the new reel came in and said, "This reel isn't working right, there doesn't seem to be much drag." The young clerk wasn't working that day, but the shop owner was, and he had to replace the reel because the little cogs that contact the drag pawl were nearly worn off. Granted, the drag system should have survived the line winding, but it didn't. Such high-speed wear and tear is easily avoided. It's a complication no one needs.

I have heard some folks say they've never had a fish take them into their backing, so they don't believe it's ever going to happen. All I can say is, someday it will happen, and then they will be sorry they didn't pay attention to this important piece of equipment. I urge all fly fishers to have plenty of backing on all the reels and spare spools they own.

My favorite knot for attaching the backing to the fly line is the very dependable nail knot. That said, you should always strip the coating from the braided core of your fly line before tying the nail knot to the fly line. The tightest coils in the nail knot are the first and last wrap of backing over the line. The top coil of backing in the nail knot is the tightest and will cut through the plastic coating of the fly line, leaving the remaining wraps not as firmly wound. It's safer to tie the nail knot directly onto the braided core of the fly line. A large fish will easily strip the fly line out of the nail knot and leave you in a sorry situation. Tie the nail knot directly to the braided core, pull it as tight as you can by gripping the tag end with a pair of pliers, wrap the backing around a leather-gloved hand, and pull hard! It's far better for something to break or fail now than on the water. Apply two or three coats of Pliobond over the knot and feather it over the fly line coating and onto the backing. This will provide a smooth junction between the two lines that won't get hung up in a snake guide or, worse yet, in the tip-top guide (which will surely snap it off).

Pay particular attention to the core of your fly line. Some do not have a braided nylon core. These lines have some type of monofilament core and a nail knot will slide off, as though it were greased. You must use an Albright knot to permanently secure the backing to this type of fly line. And you must remove the fly line coating before you begin. Coat the knot with Pliobond.

The running line on some weight-forward and multi-tip lines can be quite long. I always figure I'm going to use such lines on large rivers, lakes, or salt water and will probably need all the backing I can comfortably get on the reel without crowding the spool. A good way to determine how much running line to save is to take your rod and reel to the backyard, a lake, or a park to discover how far you can consistently and comfortably cast. Mark that spot on the running line with a Magic Marker, strip off another ten or fifteen feet, and cut off the rest of the running line. You can usually gain valuable yards of backing by doing this.

There are several methods of attaching the leader butt to the fly line, but I still prefer the nail knot. I've never had one fail in forty years of fishing. Regardless of the attachment method you use, you should always use a micrometer to measure the length of the diameter at the level end of your fly line. They all have level tips that range in length from as short as four inches to as long as fourteen or more inches. How can that happen? Fly lines are not made one at a time. They are actually made in one very long string of lines connected at their tips and butts with a level area between them. Someone or some machine cuts the lines apart and sometimes not exactly in the center of the tips. You only need four or five inches of tip section before the taper begins. Cut off anything in excess of that and attach your leader butt to the remainder. This little precaution will eliminate the possibility of a hinging effect in the end of your fly line and ensure a positive transfer of power to the leader butt section, which will improve your fly presentation dramatically. It takes just a little extra time and care to prevent later complications.

The length of the life of your fly line depends on a number of things. How long the fly line will last depends on how hard you fish, how hard you cast, how well you manage to avoid stepping on the line, and how well you maintain it. Most good quality fly lines come with a little pad of line cleaner. Use it regularly! A clean fly line will last longer and cast better than a dirty one. As a general rule, anytime you try to save a few bucks on your tackle you will end up purchasing something that is inferior to other products on the market. Granted there is some equipment on the market that appears to be a bit overpriced, but you get what you pay for in fly lines. Big savings on fly lines often means it's been on a shelf in the back room for several years.

LEADERS

When I began fly-fishing, I bought my leaders from the local fly shop. If they were out of the length and tippet strength I wanted, you can guess what that did to my attitude and my chances of fishing the way I wanted or needed. I've been playing around with different leader materials and formulas for almost as long as I've been fly-fishing. I don't buy knotless tapered leaders because I figure I'm buying something that's designed to function in the way someone else casts. They no doubt use different rods, with different actions, and fish different water than I do. Besides that, I can never know exactly what kind of taper is built into the leader without spending an hour or two measuring every inch of it. I am the kind of fisherman who needs to know the exact diameter of each section of the leader before I make my first cast. Here's why. I fish for giant brookies in Labrador on occasion and know that I'll need 3X tippet most of the time. I also want a tippet long enough to allow for stretch and probably a half dozen fly changes. To allow for that with a knotless tapered leader, I'll have to mike the leader, determine where a 2X diameter ends (and how long it is), then tie on my 3X tippet. That's way too time-consuming and complicated, so I tie my own leaders and use my own leader formula. The beauty of the formula is that it can be adjusted by anyone to suit individual casting styles and needs.

A number of leader formulas advise you to use a specific butt section diameter for a specific line weight. Don't do it. Fly lines and leader butt materials are not all the same degree of stiffness. For example, you could tie a butt section that measures .019 inch in diameter to the end of a 5-weight line and discover that the butt section is stiffer than the end of your fly line. That'll really screw up your casting. It might even happen with a butt section of .017. Horizontally hold a 5-inch length of butt section alongside an equal amount of the tip of your line between the thumb and forefinger of each hand. Slide both hands apart until you feel the end of each line under the thumb of each hand. Then, push your hands together to form a vertical loop with both pieces. If the degree of stiffness is the same, you will have two identical arcs. If the fly line bends in a sharper arc than the butt section, the butt material is too stiff. Be advised that a butt section of .019 from manufacturer A may not be as stiff as the same diameter from manufacturer B. Nor will the tip of a 5-weight line from one line maker match the degree of stiffness from another.

Use a micrometer or leader gauge to measure the diameter of each spool of leader material before purchase. Some leader materials are very accurately drawn; some are a thousandth of inch or more larger or smaller. You need to precisely know the diameter of each spool of material before you begin to build your leader. You might want to add a new section of 3X to the quick-taper portion of your leader. The spool might indicate that the leader is 3X, but if you mike it, you might find it to be 2X.

When you add on the next section of 4X, it'll become the hinge in your leader and won't transfer the loop turnover that you need. Mike all your leader spools. If they are accurately labeled, underline the designation; if not, write on the correct size with a permanent fine point marker.

With all the above in mind, I offer the leader formulas on pages 26 and 27. They are all the same design, but they begin with differing diameters of butt sections.

I use Maxima for the butt sections and quick-taper portions, then switch to Climax at 5X. I use Umpqua tippets for 6X and smaller. Some leader manufacturers have cautioned against mixing brands of leader materials, but I have found that the addition of Climax and Umpqua tippet materials works better than staying with Maxima. Knot strength doesn't seem to be affected, and the progressive limpness of the tippet materials is a near perfect match.

For spring creek angling, you often need longer leaders. The 4- to 5-weight leader starting with a .019 butt section and tied down to a 7X tippet is 11 feet 6 inches long as it is. If you opt for 5 inches of 7X and add 40 inches of 8X, you'll have a 12-foot, 4-inch leader. The leader still functions very well if 2 inches is added to each butt section and an additional inch to each quick-taper segment. This will add another 15 inches to the overall length, making it a 13-foot, 6-inch leader. And based on the design of your fly rod (fast, medium, slow action), you may need to adjust the lengths of the various segments.

I believe the reason this leader turns over so well is the gradual step down in the butt section coupled with the quick taper just before the tippet. The power of the casting loop is transmitted to the tippet in a way that compensates for the constantly diminishing line/leader diameter and the increasing limpness of the leader material. The quick-taper section performs much like squeezing a garden hose; the water speeds up as it gets restricted. A slight tug with the line hand and a little more thumb pressure during the forward cast will turn over an 18-foot leader directly into the wind! This leader design will allow you to make any fly presentation you wish simply by varying line speed.

There are a few things to remember when you're tying this leader design or any other. Never decrease the diameter of the butt sections by more than .002 inch, and never decrease by more than .001 after you have reached .009. The percentage of change in diameter increases exponentially with each .001-inch decrease. For example, the difference between .004 and .003 is 25 percent! I think it's a good idea to use a double

Typical leader formulas for 6- to 7-weight lines			Typical leader formulas for 5- to 6-weight lines		
butt section diameter		leader length	butt section diameter		leader length
.023		14 inches			
.021		14 inches	.021		14 inches
.019		14 inches	.019		14 inches
.017		14 inches	.017		14 inches
.015		10 inches	.015		14 inches
.013		9 inches	.013		10 inches
.011		8 inches	.011		9 inches
.009		7 inches	.009		8 inches
.008	(3X)	24–30 inches of tippet, or	.008		7 inches
.008		6 inches	.007		6 inches
.007	(4X)	24–30 inches of tippet, or	.006	(5X)	30 inches, or
.007		6 inches	.006		6 inches
.006	(5X)	24–30 inches	.005	(6X)	30 inches, or
			.005		5 inches
			.004	(7X)	30 inches, or
			.004		5 inches
			.003	(8X)	36 inches

Note: You may have to decrease the diameter of the first butt section of each of these leaders to match the degree of stiffness at the end of your fly line.

surgeon's knot on any tippet diameter below .005. Blood knots seem to perform adequately down to this diameter. Always lubricate every knot with saliva as you tie any leader material to another segment. There is a tremendous amount of friction heat generated as you pull the knots tight, which can seriously weaken the knot and the short section of material on either side of it. And always tug on the tag ends before clipping them off. A good way to do this is to hold the leader in both hands, grasp a tag end with your front teeth, and pull to make sure the knot is snug.

Then again, you must consider the pound strength of the tippet material available in today's market. Size 18 hooks will often bend open before a 7X tippet breaks. I used to be quite concerned with tippet strength when fishing tiny dry flies. Nowadays, I'm more concerned about how strong the hook is. It seems there are more limitations on the strength of the hook than there are on the strength of the tippet. You will not be able to land

Typical leader formulas for 4- to 5-weight lines			**Typical leader formulas for 3- to 4-weight lines**		
butt section diameter		leader length	butt section diameter		leader length
.019		16 inches			
.017		14 inches	.017		14 inches
.015		14 inches	.015		14 inches
.013		14 inches	.013		14 inches
.011		10 inches	.011		14 inches
.009		9 inches	.009		10 inches
.008		8 inches	.008		9 inches
.007		7 inches	.007		8 inches
.006	(5X)	30 inches, or	.006		7 inches
.006		6 inches	.005	(6X)	30 inches, or
.005	(6X)	30 inches, or	.005		6 inches
.005		5 inches	.004	(7X)	36 inches, or
.004	(7X)	36 inches, or	.004		5 inches
.004		5 inches	.003	(8X)	36–40 inches
.003	(8X)	36–40 inches			

every large fish you hook, especially when you're fishing fine tippets and small flies. Whenever you attempt to stop a large fish from going where it wants, you will probably break the fish off or bend the hook open. You can try to slow the fish down or guide it away from boulders and snags, but a large, determined fish will be in charge until you begin to tire it out. It's all part of the drama, fun, and enjoyment of fly fishing. I purposely choose tippet material that will break at the fly before the hook bends open. I'd sooner lose the fly than have a fly with a weakened hook in my fly box. You can bend the hook back to its original shape, but it won't be as strong. It will bend open again with less pressure.

And this brings me to a pet peeve I used to have with some fine tippets such as 6, 7, and 8X. It seemed that after I fished a while with no success, after I'd changed flies many times, the last two inches above the fly began to look like a pubic hair. There is a way to prevent this! When you thread the end of the tippet through the eye of the hook, *do not* pull the tag end of the tippet through the hook eye by pulling to one side. Most people will hold the fly in one hand, thread the tippet through the hook eye, and pull to one side to get enough tag to tie the knot. A wet tippet is soft and will flatten on one side as you pull it through the hook eye. This is what causes the curl. Pull the tippet straight through the eye putting no tension against the hook eye, somewhat like threading a needle. Push the tippet through the hook eye far enough to allow you to tie the knot with the tag end. This doesn't totally eliminate the curling problem but will greatly reduce it. It's another reason to fish with long tippets. When the curling problem gets too bad, you can cut off that portion of tippet.

There are several knots recommended for tying the fly to the tippet. My favorite is the improved clinch knot, which I use for 99 percent of my freshwater (and even most of my saltwater) fishing. I hardly ever have one fail. The secret to tying any monofilament knot is to always lubricate and pull on the tag as you are tightening the knot. I do this by touching the wraps to the end of my tongue, then grasping the tag between my teeth as I hold the fly in my left hand and pull the knot tight with my right hand. I always put the tippet through the eye of large flies such as streamers and bass bugs twice and then tie the knot. I believe there is a lot more stress and friction wear on a single strand of tippet through the eye of a large fly.

Remember that the purpose of a leader is to provide a reasonable distance between the fly line and the fly. A wary trout can be spooked by the splashdown of the leader-to-line knot just as easily as it can from a splashy fly presentation. You should be able to cast your empty leader by simply holding the butt section and casting with an arm, wrist, and hand motion. If it rolls out as if it's attached to a fly line, it's a good design.

I make an effort to always fish with the same length leader. It increases my casting accuracy immensely. For me there is some unexplainable magic about being able to judge the distance to within an inch or two on the final forward cast and see my fly land exactly where I'm looking. I'm convinced that this ability is directly related to a consistent leader length.

I just can't bring myself to fish the latest craze in leaders, the furled leader. They seem to be made from everything from 6/0 fly-tying thread to 7X tippet material. All of them require extra care if I want to fish dry flies, which is mostly what I do. A well-known personality recently showed me a furled leader of his design made of yellow 6/0 tying thread.

He told me I could attach a tippet of thirty or forty inches and it would cast beautifully. He cautioned that I would have to apply some Mucelin to make it float. Seems to me that I would be attaching a piece of uncoated line to the end of a coated line (my fly line) so that I could fasten a clear tippet to it. Why would I want to do that when I already have a leader that is clear, floats, doesn't require extra care, and separates my opaque fly line from the fly? Even if the furled leader were made of white tying thread, it would still be opaque. If it were made of 7X tippet, it would still need to be treated with Mucelin so that it would float. And both materials, because of their uneven surfaces, hold more water than monofilament. Seems to me like a step back to the days of horsehair leaders. Furled leaders may be popular with some fly fishers, but I don't think they will replace monofilament leaders.

FLIES

Now to put all your equipment and preparation to work, you must have the flies you need for the water and the fish you're going after. I usually carry enough flies to open a small streamside shop. I've been surprised too many times, so I want to be as prepared as I can be. You can find hatch charts in a number of books and magazines, and local fly shops will tell you what was working *yesterday*. Mother Nature has a habit of doing what she damn well pleases and not following our timetables. I broke down my seasonal selections in the discussion of my vest. I never vary much from these inventories, except to add a few patterns that may show up any day.

I urge you to purchase flies (if you're not a tier) from a fly shop that is near the stream where you are going to fish. They will always have the correct sizes and color variations, and they will be glad to tell you what you'll need. Even if you tie your own flies, it's a good idea to buy one of each fly the local shop recommends just to make sure you get it right as you tie them. Try to get some photos of the naturals that live in the water you'll be fishing. The profiles, proportions, and colors of the materials will be much more accurate than most of the flies you can purchase.

For my dries, I dislike fly boxes that have any clips, flat foam, or foam ridges to hold the flies in place because the hackles get smashed, their capacity is limited, and they usually aren't designed for a variety of hook sizes. I like to carry all my BWO flies, from size 16 down to 26, in one box. I have found that a compartment box fits my needs best because I can carry both duns and parachutes in the same box, each in a separate row. I have a twelve-compartment box that allows me to carry BWOs from size 16 to 26. I try to fill my fly boxes with specific hatches so that, when I stock my vest, all I have to do is take the fly boxes that contain the flies for a specific season or stream.

Nymphs and streamers are another matter. I use nothing but flat styrofoam-lined boxes for nymphs and streamers. If the box has no ventilating holes, I drill some small holes in the sides of the box to prevent the hooks from rusting. I carry a minimum of streamers that includes olive and black Wooly Buggers, gold Muddlers, Black-Nose Dace, and Clouser Mickey Finns. The nymph box is loaded with Gold-Ribbed Hare's Ears (both weighted and unweighted), Pheasant Tails, midge larva (in four colors), a few stonefly nymphs, some Soft-Hackled Hare's Ears, and Quill-Body RS-2s in four colors.

Special trips often require some special flies. When I fish in Canada, many of the hatches in the nearby provinces are much like those in Colorado. Always contact someone in the area you intend to fish about hatches and hook sizes. Learn the laws regarding weighted flies and leaders. It's illegal in some places in the United States and Canada to fish with any kind of weight on your tippet. This is important information for anyone who is fishing nymphs and streamers. You'll need sinking tip lines with short leaders, a multi-tip line or several lengths of lead core trolling line, and weighted flies. Never leave home without your Olive Quill Duns and Parachutes. There are good hatches of BWOs in sizes 14 to 20 in many places throughout the world. Most fly-fishing lodges include hatch chart information with the other materials they send you prior to the trip. If you can get the name of a guide, contact him or her to find out what you will need and what to expect.

3

Care of Your Gear

It's most important to take good care of both the reel and the line because if either fails to function properly, you'll have a miserable day. Taking care of the other parts of your gear is just as important if you want to prevent and avoid complications.

One such complication is having the tip section of your rod sail along with your line on the final forward cast. If you're fishing a tiny fly when this happens, you'll probably lose the rod tip and the rest of the day's fishing. Of all the sickening feelings, this has to be among the worst. The good news is it can easily be prevented. Losing a tip section is usually caused by not paying attention to the ferrule fit between the butt and tip sections. Graphite rod ferrules need to be treated with some kind of paraffin product such as a candle. Use a clean, soft cloth to clean the male part of the ferrule, squeezing firmly and twisting back and forth to remove any dust or dirt particles that invariably adhere to it. It's the dirt and dust that will eventually remove tiny amounts of the ferrule each time you assemble your rod, eventually causing the ferrules to become loose. I then apply one or two strokes of paraffin to the length of the male ferrule, buff it off with a soft cloth, and then reapply. Don't overdo it by trying to coat every tiny bit of the ferrule. Some graphite rods have a spigot male ferrule. When this rod is assembled, there may be as much as a quarter inch of space between the two rod sections. Do not try to force the male ferrule all the way into the female portion, or you'll have one hell of a time getting the pieces apart, or worse yet, you'll ruin the female portion of the ferrule. You might think the male part of the ferrule is too long, but not so. The male spigot is made longer on purpose to compensate for the wear factor. Use a Q-Tip to clean the female portion of the ferrule. Then, when you assemble your rod, insert the male ferrule into the female while aligning the guides at about an 11:00 position from the female guides. When the connection begins to feel firm, twist the tip into alignment with the rest of the rod, continuing to push the two pieces together with only a little pressure. The twisting motion will lock the two ferrules together. This is best done in one uninterrupted motion. To remove the tip after a day's fishing, simply twist the tip back toward the 11:00 position as you pull the two pieces away from each other.

Assembling bamboo rods is another matter entirely. Never twist the sections of a cane rod as you assemble it. Always align the guides before pushing the ferrules straight toward each other. Put the butt section under one armpit and grip it with your hand as close to the ferrule as possible. Grasp the tip section near the ferrule with your other hand and push the two together. Never twist the sections of a cane rod as you take it apart. Position each hand as close to the ferrules as possible and pull straight away. This is best done by tucking the butt section under an armpit and locking your wrist next to your chest. Use your other hand to push straight away from you. But before you begin, make absolutely sure you are standing in an open area. You need at least six feet of open space in front of you or you'll jam the tip into someone's chest, a tree, or your truck. Stationary objects seem to move closer as you pull a cane rod apart.

Stubborn ferrules on a cane rod can be a problem, but one that is easily solved if you carry two six- to eight-inch lengths of bicycle inner tube in your vest. Cut off two six- to eight-inch lengths of tube, split them down the center, and trim away about half of each one. You will then have two strips that are about two inches wide. Place each piece of inner tube lengthwise on either side of the ferrules for a more secure handgrip.

You can also use these strips to untwist stuck graphite ferrules. They provide a no-slip grip that will not damage your rod's finish.

Never lubricate a metal ferrule. Good ferrules are usually made of German nickel silver, a material that has lubricative qualities of its own when it's kept perfectly clean. Oils or paraffin on metal will only hasten its wear. Both oil and paraffin collect microscopic particles of dust that function as a fine abrasive each time you assemble and disassemble your rod. The ferrules will wear down quickly, and that's how you can lose the tip of the rod.

Clean cane ferrules frequently. I use a soft cotton cloth with a few drops of denatured alcohol on the cloth to buff the male ferrule clean. Then I dip a Q-Tip into the alcohol and swab out the inside of the female ferrule. Clean both ferrules until they no longer produce any gray-looking deposit on the Q-Tip or the cloth. You must be extremely careful that you do not allow any of the alcohol to come in contact with the thread wraps on either ferrule or you'll damage the fine varnish finish.

Some old cane rods may have ferrules that have become a little sloppy in their fit simply because they have been used a lot. Things do wear down with extended use. If you notice that your tip section begins to rotate to one side as you are fishing, you need to get that rod to an expert repairman for a ferrule adjustment. If you can't afford or don't want to have the ferrules replaced, an experienced rod repairman can squeeze the male portion in a three-jawed chuck, and the rod will be good for many more years before the ferrules need to be replaced. Maybe you feel brave enough to make the adjustment yourself. If you've never done it before, my advice is don't try it. It's really easy to ruin both the ferrule and the rod.

If you can't resist making the repair, be certain that each of the three jaws is in perfect alignment with three of the flats (sides) of the rod. Use a chuck key to tighten the chuck slightly, then loosen the chuck, remove the rod tip from the chuck, and try the fit. Repeat until you can feel that it's better than when you began. The chuck squeeze puts three microscopic dents in the ferrule over three of the flats, while at the same time putting a slight bulge in the areas over the remaining three flats, essentially making the male ferrule a little fatter in three places. But, the contact inside the female ferrule will now be in only three places, which means the ferrule may wear out much faster. It's a one-time fix, and you probably should practice this on a rod that's not worth much money before you try it on your treasure.

I always wipe my rods, both graphite and cane, with a clean, soft cloth after a day of fishing. It gets all the water marks off the glassy finish and allows a quick inspection of every inch of the rod. I stand the cane sections in a safe corner to dry overnight before I put them back in the tube. If you've been fishing salt water, you must thoroughly hose the rod and reel with fresh water and wipe them as dry as possible. It's a good idea to leave the graphite sections out overnight as well, just to give the cork grip a chance to dry out before you put it in an airtight tube where it will surely get moldy otherwise. I like reels that have quick-release spools because it allows me to thoroughly wash both the spool and the frame.

Salt water has a way of corroding just about every metal object that we use. It's a good idea to wash your flies too.

Check out the leader butt and line connection before each trip. That portion of the line tip immediately in front of the leader butt will often develop a crack that makes a wonderful hinge in your forward cast. If exposed, the line core will soak up water in only a few minutes. This crack is often caused because the Pliobond coating over the junction wasn't feathered up on the line tip far enough or you didn't take the time to do it when you attached your leader butt to the fly line. Use a little Pliobond to paint a thin coat over the crack. Let it dry and apply another coat. Other cracks may appear in your line. You may get some while fishing on a windy day or when your casting timing isn't quite perfect and the leader tippet wraps itself around the line with enough force that it actually cuts into the line coating. Simply apply a couple of coats of thin Pliobond to these places to prevent the coating from peeling from the core.

As long as you are checking your line for cracks, you should carefully examine the entire leader. Lightly grip the leader with your thumb and forefinger and gently pull it through to determine if there are any nicks or overhand knots. Replace any portion of the leader that has a knot or nick in it. Both will dramatically weaken your leader and cause it to fail at precisely the wrong time. If you tie your own leaders, you can replace only the section that needs it and not the entire leader.

Thoroughly hose both the inside and outside of your wading shoes as soon as you can after fishing. One of my pet peeves is that some wading shoes will shrink when they get dry. I haven't been able to figure out how it's possible for something that's made of synthetic material to shrink, but mine do. It's one more little detail to take care of before I leave the house. I soak the shoes with a garden hose and put them in a large plastic bag and pack them in my duffle with my waders and vest. They'll still be wet when I get to the stream, but I haven't soaked anything else along the way. The plastic bag serves the same purpose on the way home. It's a good idea to hose the outside of your waders. Allow all wet items to dry completely before you store them. I hang my waist-high breathables by the belt from a hook I put in a corner of my storage room. The only part of a pair of breathable waders that gets damp while you're fishing is the insides of the neoprene stocking feet. Hanging them from the belt allows the inside to dry in only a few hours.

And don't forget to throw those smelly and matted wool socks in the laundry. Your feet will stay warmer and dryer much longer if your wool socks are clean.

4

The Approach

The manner in which you approach the water before you even make the first cast will often set you up for the kind of day you're going to have. It doesn't matter if you're fishing a spring creek, small stream, river, pond, or lake. It's possible to blow your entire day with a clumsy approach.

There's a kind of a mind game you have to play with yourself or your mind will play games with you all day and you'll go home frustrated. It goes like this. The first trout you see is the most important fish of the day, and it could be lying exactly where you intend to step into the water. I feel like a fool when I spook a fish because I didn't look carefully before I got close to the water's edge. It's a feeling that hangs on, is there in the back of my mind, and prevents me from gaining an edge or the feeling that I'm "on." It's a sickening feeling that won't go away.

If you spot a rising fish on the other side of the stream, resist the temptation to go charging out to a casting position without looking around on *your* side of the stream, especially if your side of the stream is shady. Oftentimes, the larger trout is the one you spook when you get in the water. Trout *do* live on both sides of a stream! In spite of what anyone says about where trout like to be, they can be anyplace they choose. As a general rule, they'll tend to hang out in places where food comes to them, where they feel relatively safe and don't have to work very hard to stay there. That could be anyplace between the two banks.

There's a choice you need to make when you arrive at the place you intend to fish. Do you carefully walk down to the water's edge to see if there are any rising fish and take the chance of spooking the big one hanging near the bank? Or do you string up your rod and put on all your gear first? I've done it both ways. The problem I've had with going to look without the rod is that if I do see rising fish, I invariably miss a guide in my haste to string up my rod, drop an open box of flies, forget to put on the gravel guards before I put my boots on, or worse yet, tie a sloppy tippet knot. I try to make myself accomplish all the gearing up before I approach the water, including straightening the leader and tippet. By the way, I suggest you throw away that little thing sold in fly shops called a leader straightener. Every one of them will ruin your leader and especially the tippet. You'll generate a tremendous amount of heat as you pull your leader through this straightener. Your leader will be straight all right, but it will be much weaker from the heat damage. To straighten your leader, hold it firmly between the heel of your thumb and all four fingertips as you pull it through this grip. You'll burn the heel of your thumb before you ruin your leader.

A safe way to straighten your leader.

Stringing up the rod with a loop of fly line.

String up your rod by doubling over about twelve inches of the tip of your fly line and threading it through each of the guides. It's a good way to prevent having to start all over again should you lose your grip on the line. The doubled loop will stop itself at the first guide below it.

Pull about two feet of line and leader butt through the tip-top guide and execute a quick backcast followed by a quick forward cast. The entire leader will go out through all the guides. Tie on a fly and wind line onto your reel until there's about a foot of the tip of the fly line out of the tip-top guide. Loop the leader around the reel and hook the fly in one of the guides; then tighten the line by gently winding line back onto the reel. Always try to leave about a foot of the tip of the fly line out of the tip-top guide. This will prevent putting a kink in the butt section of the leader and makes extending line before the first cast much easier. I never use that little loop of wire called a hook keeper unless I'm using a leader that's shorter than the rod.

String up your rod well away from the stream while keeping an eye on the water to see if there are any rising fish. If there are none, take note

Leader around the reel frame and spool prevents a kink in the leader butt.

of the bankside vegetation. Look for overhanging trees, bushes, or long grass. Look for shelves and drop-offs and current creases. Try to determine if there are any underwater weeds, water-soaked logs, or submerged boulders. Trout love to hang out in these places because there's cover for them and also many insects and baitfish.

Approach the water's edge cautiously, holding your rod horizontal with the tip to the rear. If you're using a 9-foot rod and you point the shiny tip forward as you approach, you could spook a fish and not even know it.

Scan the edge of the stream both left and right as you slowly move forward. If you are the first person to the water, you'll often find fish hanging out near the shoreline looking for an easy meal of terrestrials. Slowly walk well away from the water's edge toward the spot you intend to fish. Your boot falls should make no more sound than your shadow! Watch a great blue heron stalking its prey and you'll get the idea. And by all means, dress in earthtone colors. No white T-shirts, yellow straw hats, or white ball caps. Trout will see you coming before you get close enough to cast. Dress like a predator, not like an advertisement for some T-shirt company.

A perfect example of a grassy undercut bank.
There's a trout under there someplace.

The shiny tip of my
tip-top guide just
spooked a nice trout
right in front of me.

Try to dress to blend in with the background foliage.

Examine the bushes, trees, and grass for spider webs and take note of the kinds of insects you see trapped there. Gently tap bushes and tree branches with your rod tip to see if you can disturb resting insects. Carefully examine the streamside to see if wave action, currents, or wind has deposited any insects there. Look in the air above the stream to determine if there are any mayflies or caddis in the air and try to judge their size and color. Learn all you can from the clues before you tie on your first fly, and then tie on the fly that matches the insects that seem most prevalent.

A strong wind is not good for fly casting, but it could make your day if the winds are blowing grasshoppers, ants, and beetles into the stream. If it's too early in the season for hoppers, tie on a size 16 or 18 beetle or ant and cast to likely holding spots along the bank near brush, logs, and rocks.

Many streams have some kind of weed growth, and that is where you'll find a lot of aquatic insects. Grab a handful of weeds or moss and carefully observe what's crawling around in it. Stream bottoms vary a great deal in their makeup. Sometimes you'll find a mucky area, but usually bottoms are sandy and gravelly with small rocks and boulders as well. Shuffle your feet a couple of times and use your bug net to capture

Typical green drake hatch on Colorado's Frying Pan River.

These little worms are trout food and should not be ignored.

This nymph tells me what size and color nymph pattern to use.

any nymphs or larvae you may have disturbed. Pick up a rock to see what's crawling around under it. You could find the primary food source by doing these things. Sometimes there is so much bug life on the stream bottom that I feel guilty that I may be squashing hundreds of bugs with each step.

When I arrive at a stream, I have to make some choices that are sometimes difficult. If the stream is crowded with other fly fishers, I drive on down- or upstream until I find a parking area with only one or two cars. Sometimes I have to drive more than I'd like, but one of the main reasons I like to fish is for the solitude that fishing provides. When the stream is crowded, another option is to fish the water that no one likes to fish. All the "good" spots are taken: The riffles, runs, and pools that everyone seems to know hold fish and where the casting is relatively easy are occupied. There is always some heavy (deeper and faster) water someplace near these hot spots, and you can bet that's where the bigger fish will be holding. They've been driven there by all the activity in the easy places. Game will always seek refuge from predators, and in a stream, that's the heavy water, the water that's not easy to wade or fish. It might take a little thought and ingenuity, but usually there is a way you can manage to fish it.

There is usually a high-bank deep side and a shallow side to these heavy water places. The runs are narrow and deep and filled with boulders or large rocks. I always walk downstream until I can find a spot to cross the stream to get to the shallow side at the tail of a wide pool. Wade across by staying just below the lower edge of the pool. This will prevent any shock waves from traveling up into the pool as you cross. You may have to walk around a fly fisher or two fishing the pool. Simply walk slowly and well away from the water's edge, which will tell the people already there that you have no intention of infringing on their territory, but keep your eyes on the stream as much as you can as you slowly walk upstream. If you spot a fish or two, make a mental note of their location and keep going. Walk upstream until you get to the head of the run, and then sit down and take a ten-minute break. Try to believe that all the trout in front of you know you're there. Spend these few minutes deciding what to do next. Did you find out what's been hatching in the last few days? Were there any bugs in the air while you were walking upstream? See anything on the water? Did you notice any boulders or sunken logs? Did you see any dead water either in front of or behind them? How long were the current creases? If you were paying attention to all these things, you will be able to decide what fly to tie on and where to cast it.

Heavy water. Drop a heavily weighted nymph into the white water to sink down quickly to the dark water, where a trout may be hiding.

I always fish areas like this from a position that will allow me to make a cast downstream at a 30-degree angle to place the fly a foot or two above where I think a trout might be holding or where I saw a rise. The current is usually quite strong and a longer float will create drag on the fly just as it approaches the intended drift. These holding spots are often only two or three feet long. Trout don't have much time to decide if they want the fly. As soon as your fly is past where you think a fish is holding, lift the fly and, with only one backcast, put it back on the water. You may occasionally find that there is another holding spot just a few feet below your first choice. If that is the case, strip some line from the reel and wiggle the rod tip to work out the line to extend the drift. This will allow you to fish two possible lies with one cast. Don't give up after twelve or fifteen drifts! The biggest brook trout I ever caught in the Frying Pan River (a 20-incher) came up and ate the fly on the twentieth cast. And, it came up from a depth of thirty inches! I landed it a block downstream. Of course, this frantic chase downstream spooked all the other fish in the stretch, but that monster was worth it. After landing it and taking a dozen photos of it laying in three inches of water, I slowly walked back upstream and sat down for ten minutes before I began fishing the rest of the run. And I caught more fish! When fish are on the feed, they will usually begin rising again in ten or fifteen minutes. The thing to remember here is that I was fishing a spot that few fly fishers want to try. It's my belief that the trout in such places aren't so easily put down for longer periods because they haven't been bothered much. And since the surface is usually broken by more wave action from the stronger currents, the trout can't see me as easily. Many fly fishers think heavy water is difficult fishing because of the narrow channel and swift current. It's actually easier than trying to get a dead drift on a mirror smooth pool. The casts are usually shorter, which means you can be more accurate, and since the drifts are shorter, you can present your fly to the same fish more often. That was a memorable day for me because on that day I joined the exclusive Frying Pan club, the 20-inch Full House Club. I hooked and landed a 20-inch brook, rainbow, brown, and native cutthroat trout on the same fly! In water that no one wanted to fish. The piscatorial gods were smiling on me that day. It hasn't happened again and I don't expect it to, but I do still fish that run every year.

Stand on the bank and make your first few casts upstream to present the fly in any likely holding spot no matter how shallow or fast the water

Casting to shallow, rocky water. Look carefully and you can see my white fly where a trout should be resting.

Notice the white fly in the current crease on the far side of this current chute.

may appear to be. Gradually make casts that present the fly to deeper holding places until you are fishing the middle of the current.

Take a step forward now and then as you extend the distance you are casting until you can comfortably cast to the current creases on the other side of the stream. As you are working your way out into deeper water, watch those areas both in front of and behind any kind of subsurface cover to see if you can spot a fish. Oftentimes there will be a slick in these places that acts as a sort of window to the bottom.

If you see a fish, watch it for a while to see what it's doing. You can often see fish moving about near the bottom as they feed on passing nymphs. This is the ideal time to do a little sight fishing with a nymph. My first choice of a nymph pattern in a case like this is a size 18 Gold-Ribbed Hare's Ear or Pheasant Tail. I fish only one fly at a time. I've tried fishing a brace of nymphs and must admit that the tactic works, but I experience many more foul-hooked fish when I fish a two-nymph rig. Besides, I prefer to catch trout one at a time. The best way to avoid foul-hooking a fish when you're fishing a two-nymph rig is to use a longer leader between the two flies. Eighteen inches should be the minimum length.

It's a good bet that there is a trout holding in front of this boulder.

Sometimes a run can be a block or two long and contain stretches of pocket water and riffles before it begins to slow and widen into everyone's favorite pool. Carefully scan the riffle water and the pocket water behind boulders and rocks. Both areas will have a rhythm to their surfaces. If you notice anything that seems out of rhythm, you can bet it was a rise. The best method to use in scanning such areas is to not let your eyes rest on any specific area for more than a second. Sweep back and forth as you notice small eddies and minute current creases. The wave action in both these areas and between them will have a definite undulating pattern. If you notice anything that remotely resembles a rise, it probably was. But watch that spot for a few minutes to see if it happens on a regular basis, which might indicate it is caused by the current. If the movement is sporadic, it's probably a trout.

When I spot rises in pocket water, I will usually cut my leader back to add some 5X tippet and tie on a highly visible pattern such as a Royal Wulff, Caddis, or Parachute in an appropriate size. I want to be able to easily see my fly, and tippet sizes smaller than 5X simply can't handle the speed and strength of most fish I hook in pocket water. The best tactic I have found for fishing pocket water is to cast upstream using no more than two or three feet of line and the leader. This allows me to keep all but a foot or two of tippet off the water and eliminates surface drag to almost nothing. Keep the rod tip high and present the fly to a likely holding spot at least a half dozen times before moving up to the next pocket. Pocket water trout seem eager to eat a fly. I think that's because they don't have much time to look it over. They'll eat anything that remotely looks like an insect and immediately spit it out if it isn't. Your reaction to the strike must be immediate!

I always use a wading staff when fishing pocket water. The water can be very fast, almost treacherous, and I don't want to stumble and fall in such a place because I'm afraid I'll break something if I do.

A beautiful pocket between boulders.

Fishing riffle water is a little more relaxed because you can approach the rising fish from the side, and you don't have to be all that concerned about your footing. There is usually more than just one fish feeding in the riffles, and since the current speed is more or less constant over a wider area, you can place your casts to pick off the risers at the bottom and your side of the riffle first. You can get quite close to rising fish in both pocket water and riffle water because the surface is broken enough that the trout can't see you until you're almost on top of them. It can be a hell of a lot of fun, but you must be able to drop your fly on a dime-size area no more than a foot or two upstream of the fish. When fishing riffle water, just as it is in pocket water, it's important to keep as much line and leader as possible off the water. Even a little bit of drag will alarm the trout. Riffle water trout can be just as selective as stillwater trout. Net the water and tie on a fly that matches what you find. A parachute version of the hatch is my first choice. But a hackled spinner can be deadly.

My favorite rod for this type of fishing is an 8½-foot 5-weight rod with a 12-foot leader tapered to 5X. I like this arrangement because I can often keep most of the leader off the water to reduce drag to almost nothing. A well-designed leader is mandatory for fishing riffles and other short-line situations.

Sometimes you get lucky, and there's not a car in the parking spot near your favorite place to fish. Aren't you glad you remembered to pack a sandwich and a few munchies along with a canteen of water in the back of your vest? The fishing spot I have in mind contains all the attributes of all my favorite places to fish. The place where I usually enter the water is halfway up the run and is shallow and sandy and scattered with some small rocks and limestone flakes. The stream above and to my left is a braided chute with some boulders, most of which aren't much larger than a basketball. The current flows in the main channel near the far side, and its bank is lined with overhanging willows and alders interspersed with a few areas of overhanging grass and slightly undercut banks. On the far side there are a few groups of rocks whose tops are either visible or just barely submerged. The current starts to slow as the stream begins to widen and becomes a little less treacherous to wade. It eventually spreads into a wide flat pool before it begins another tumble through the next chute. There is an overhanging tree to my left, hardly a rod's length away, and I've always noticed a few trout under it. Just upstream from the tree is a little current braid right next to the bank that is slightly undercut with overhanging grass. A couple of nice trout hold there. To the right is a large

Good-looking riffle water with lots of holding places and broken surfaces.

boulder that splits the current and not only produces the little current braid to its left but also creates a two-foot-deep channel with a wonderfully swift current crease nearly twenty feet long. The resident rainbows love this place and are eager to charge up to eat a buggy-looking dry. To the right of the swift crease is the main channel that is so fast that the surface is almost glassy smooth. It's water you can't stand up in if you're in up to your waist. Thigh deep works, but you'd better have a wading staff because it's really tricky to get back out. Then, as the current begins to slow a little toward the far side, there are a few smaller rocks and a couple of current creases created by more rocks and an underwater ledge. The stream gradually begins to shallow out as the pool gets wider and smoother.

Downstream to my right the current is slower and shallow, with willows eight to ten feet high that provide shade for a distance of three to six feet from a grassy bank. There are always a few small trout hanging out there, sipping ants and beetles and the occasional spinner. These fish are seldom more than twelve inches long in water that is only about a foot deep, but they are just as selective as the larger ones elsewhere and easily spooked.

I know of such a place, and it's my all-time favorite spot to fish because it's full of casting challenges and brown and rainbow trout that can

This is my all-time favorite place to fly-fish.

tape twenty inches or more. The mayfly hatches are prolific, and there are caddis, stoneflies, and midges as well. It's almost the perfect run: a twelve-foot-wide whitewater riffle breaking into a six-foot-wide chute that mellows out to a thirty-yard-long pool that gradually slows, then breaks into another whitewater riffle. Any casting problem you could find on any stream in the country can be found in this wonderful stretch of water. Most people fish the pool at the tail of the run because it is a classic dry-fly pool where you can make long, lazy casts to rising fish almost anyplace in it. The big guys are upstream in the heavier water. There really is such a place, and of course, I'm not going to tell you where it is.

I will sometimes approach this spot from the lip of the pool at the bottom of the run and stand in front of the willows in the smooth water before it breaks over the rocky ridge that crosses the stream from one side to the other. The willows, which begin to curve around behind me with the narrowing stream, break up my silhouette. Standing in this spot will help to prevent the faster current from applying drag to my cast more quickly than I can pick up the line as it breaks over the rocks. I begin my fishing here if I see rising fish because I can fish the entire run in a clockwise direction. If there are no rising fish, I'll walk upstream and begin just below the tree that hangs out over the river.

5

Casting Techniques

When I begin fishing the bottom of the ideal run I described in the previous chapter, I'll choose a position that allows me to present an upstream cast to a rising trout at about an angle of 10 or 20 degrees to the current. With such a cast my dry fly floats downstream without any of my tippet floating over the fish's nose before the fly gets there. Fishing at that angle keeps the splash of line and leader far enough away from the fish so it won't be spooked. The surface is quite smooth here, so I try to make the cast with an open loop that will still have enough power behind it to unroll the leader in gentle S curves. A slight sidearm cast will often provide just enough of a left hook to put the tippet well away from the fish.

It's a little tricky to fish this spot because the current speed increases between my fly and me, decreasing the length of a drag-free drift as I get farther from the bank. Casting accuracy and line mending are required in such situations.

I try to wade as stealthily as a heron so I don't send any shock waves as I move forward or to one side. It's always a good idea in a situation like this to do all your false casting and line lengthening far to one side of the fish and keep the forward loops as low to the water as possible.

Sometimes it's a good idea to execute the false casts very high so that the willows hide the fly line as it flies back and forth.

Upstream 10:00 angle cast to place the leader to one side of the trout.

Mending line upstream to increase the length of a drag-free float.

False-casting low to the water to keep the line and fly out of the fish's view.

False-casting high above the willows to hide the line and fly from the trout.

Roll-casting to midstream to lengthen the line in preparation for the final forward cast.

Oftentimes, I'll roll-cast several times toward the middle of the stream to extend the line and then make the final presentation cast with no false-casting near the fish.

It usually takes me three or four casts to finally put the fly over the fish where I'd like it to land. But I'm a believer in presenting the first few casts to a spot that will be at least a foot or two to my side of the fish. If the fish is really hungry, it'll often charge over to grab the fly. If it doesn't, I can gradually work the fly in closer to the fish's holding spot and get better floats as I adjust the angle of my casting arm and the power of the cast for more dramatic left hooks.

I'll work the bankside run as far as I can with comfortable fifteen- to twenty-five-foot casts upstream and to the left. But before I lengthen my casts I'll try to gradually work the little dry fly in tight to the bank just in case there is a fish that I can't see under the shady willows. Getting a fly under low-hanging willows or any other kind of brush can be almost impossible from my standing position. And it's a good way to lose a lot of flies. I'm not one who can execute all the fancy "on-my-knees sidearm casts" that I've seen the experts demonstrate to shoot a fly for fifteen feet a few inches above the water. Once in a while, when I'm really on, I can get a fly to skip under the low, overhanging brush by overpowering a low sidearm cast. It takes a little practice to make a skip cast work because you have to aim the fly to hit the water immediately under the over-hanging branch with enough sidearm force to cause it to skip back under the brush. The fly actually hits the water behind a short loop of line and leader, which picks up the fly and throws it back under the brush. To make this work, the casting loop must be in a near horizontal position with the fly trailing lower than the loop. If the angle isn't just right, you'll drive the fly into the water with a hell of a splash of leader and line and scare the fish. It's a little like skipping a flat pebble with a string attached. I'm always afraid the splash the fly makes as it skips back into the dark spaces will spook whatever is in there.

The skip cast. Look carefully and you can see where the leader and fly hit the water and were pulled forward by the fly line loop in front.

Good example of a high open loop to drop a fly in a vertical opening in the bankside brush.

When making a pile cast, I look for a little vertical channel of air between the branches. This isn't an easy cast because the forward line and leader loop must perfectly match the gap in the foliage or you'll catch one of the branches to either side. The slightest breeze can mean trouble. This cast is best made with a rather open loop so that, if the fly does come in contact with a leaf or branch, chances are it'll dribble down to the surface much like a natural that has lost its grip.

If I can't find an open channel between branches, I'll make a few roll casts toward the center of the stream as I gradually sidestep upstream. I move into a position that will allow me to make an across-and-downstream cast to drift the fly downstream under the willow branches, after I've fished the easier water just under the outside edge of the overhanging brush.

I'm always a little surprised that I occasionally get a few strikes out in the middle of the stream with my roll casts. I can spend two hours fishing no more than twenty feet of stream without getting to the other side, where the big trout hang out. The first hour or two spent doing this is a warm-up for what is ahead. I see it as a chance to try a few patterns, net the water to see what I can find, and check out my casting ability. Some days I cast better than other days. And if there are a few little trout rising in a place like this, isn't it a good idea to try to catch them just in case someday a hog is in there? If I'm successful, I'll have a much better chance of fooling the big fish because I know what to do to get a good drift in a tough spot.

My favorite rod for fishing this kind of water (and the entire run) is an 8½-foot for a 5-weight line. My favorite rod happens to be bamboo, and I use it in almost every trout fishing situation. It's a 2-piece rod with a butt section strong enough to turn heavy rainbows in whitewater, yet the upper butt and tip are delicate enough to cast eighteen feet of leader with forty inches of 7X tippet and a size 24 dry fly. It's the Gierach-Best taper that Mike Clark of Lyons, Colorado, makes. I'm convinced that someday this model will become known as Mike's finest work. It'll do everything I ask of it, from casting directly into the wind with tiny fourteen-inch loops,

A down-and-across presentation to get the fly under the overhanging brush.

nymphing with a brace of weighted nymphs, or throwing weighted size 6 and 8 streamers to the far bank. It's almost as if the flies have eyes when I fish this wonderful rod. I have a bunch of cane rods, but this one stands in front of the stack where I can reach it without moving the others.

I think that rods shorter than 8 feet have some built-in handicaps for streams wider than ten or twelve feet. Since mending line seems to be essential in almost every fishing situation I encounter, the longer rod allows me to lift more line from the water to toss an up- or downstream loop to extend drifts. A longer rod allows me to keep my backcast above the willows and other bankside brush, and I can lean a cast to either side of my body.

What I call a lean cast comes close to being a reach cast, which is usually made across and slightly up- or downstream by sweeping the rod either right or left just after delivering the forward cast and before the fly lands on the water. This action places the fly line up- or downstream of the main current. I like to think of the reach cast as something I do because I can't or am too lazy to move upstream or down two or three steps. It's a great way to extend a drag-free drift.

High backcast above the willows behind me.

Reach cast to the upstream side.

I use a lean cast when I've already waded way too deep. To get a proper drift I need to stretch my casting arm far to the right or left as I false-cast (no, I can't cast left-handed) in order to lay the fly line in a section of current that won't drag the fly downstream faster than the current where the fly is. This can often happen when I'm fishing almost straight up- or downstream.

Upstream lean cast to get the fly line to land in the current crease so both fly and fly line come downstream at the same speed.

Downstream lean cast to get the fly and the fly line to land in the current crease so both go downstream at the same speed.

Upstream lean casts are a little easier for hooking a rising trout than downstream casts. In downstream casts the leader tends to straighten way too fast and cause drag, or worse yet, the leader straightens just as the fly comes to a riser. When the fish comes up to suck in the fly, the tightness of the leader prevents it from moving. A good way to stop this from happening is to give the rod a little jiggle as the line is still in the air on the forward cast. The jiggle will produce a bunch of shallow S curves in both the line and leader, which will allow me to strip line from the reel and continue to jiggle the rod as the fly comes within striking range of the fish. The challenge I have in this situation is being able to quickly set up when a fish does take the fly because of all the S curves in the fly line. Since the fly can't move until everything is straight, I try to be careful how big the S curves are.

Upstream lean cast to present a fly in front of a boulder.

Another situation that might require a lean cast is when you're be-hind a boulder and wish to present a fly either upstream or down. The current coming around the boulder will create faster currents that fan away from the boulder for some distance downstream. Study these cur-rents carefully and use the lean cast to get your fly and line to land in the middle of the current.

Another cast I have found to be very useful in some situations is one I call painting. Like the reach cast, the rod is swept to either side after the forward cast is made. Keep the rod tip high on the final forward cast and gently swing it to one side and down to about a 2:30 or 10:30 position immediately after the fly hits the water. The fly will hit the water before any leader or line, and at that very moment sweep the rod to one side to paint the line either upstream or down as the situation may require. It's much like a curved brush stroke in painting. The difficulty with this cast is getting the fly to hit the water exactly where you want and stay there.

Painting the fly line upstream after the fly has landed on the water.

Sometimes, making the painting move with the rod will drag the fly away from where I want it to stay. That usually happens if I give too much effort to sweeping the rod to one side. It should be a gentle motion. If there is even a slight breeze, this cast is extremely difficult to execute because the moving air will often sweep the line farther than I want. This one requires perfect timing and feels so good when everything goes right.

Whenever I use the lean, reach, or painting cast, I try to get the fly to land three or four feet above the fish I've targeted. In the time it takes for the fly to float down to the fish I can strip a little more line from the reel and flip the extra line upstream or down to lengthen the float.

You can make all these casts with an 8-foot rod if you're fishing rivers from eight to twenty feet wide, but an 8½- or 9-foot rod is ideal. It doesn't seem like much, but an additional six to twelve inches on the rod can make a world of difference in handling line after the forward cast is made. I believe too many fly fishers think the cast is over when the fly hits the water. It's only the beginning. It's what you do with the line after the fly hits the water that completes the cast. The cast is over when you pick up the line to make another cast.

And that brings me to some advice about picking up or retrieving line during the drift. Once you have determined the length of line you need to present the fly to a specific area, try to keep as much of the retrieved line in your line hand as possible. I've seen fly fishers with as much as ten yards of line flowing downstream in a big loop.

Then, when they pick up the line and fly to make another cast, they have to make three or four false casts to regain control of the line and its speed to make another cast. All this time the fly is in the air and not on the water. Keep as much line as possible in your line hand, lower the rod tip to the surface, and as you quickly raise the rod tip, yank the line toward you with your line hand with a very quick tug. Allow some line to shoot during the backcast, change the rod direction toward your target area, execute a sharp forward cast, and shoot the remainder of the line during the forward cast. This is impossible to do with a long loop of line hanging in the water. This pickup and forward cast will always present the fly a little farther upstream than you intended, so you must aim for a spot that is about two or three feet below where you really want the fly to land. Like everything else in fly fishing, it takes a little practice. Generally speaking, your fly will go where your thumb is pointing. (I learned that by listening to Lefty Kreh and, as always, he's right about it.) To finish

A long loop of line trailing downstream is trouble waiting to happen.

A vertical casting loop is mandatory for perfect casting accuracy.

this cast you must apply a little reach technique to throw the line up- or downstream of the main current between you and the fly. If I need to really drop the fly on a dime, I usually make one false forward cast to make sure the direction of the fly and line is absolutely perfect; then I shoot the extra line to put the fly into a very tight area. This is best accomplished by keeping the rod and line loop as vertical as possible. Some-

The roll cast pickup saves retrieving a lot of line and minimizes false casting.

times, especially when fishing midge adults, we need to place the fly so that it will float down to the trout in line with the middle of its nose. Trout won't usually move very far to either side to eat a tiny midge.

Sometimes you simply must cast upstream. It's almost mandatory when you're fishing small streams where there is no room to stand to one side or when you are fishing pocket water in a little mountain stream. Maintaining line control is crucial in either case. Both situations are good times to use a roll cast pickup before you make your next forward cast. It's really easy to do. Execute the beginning of a roll cast, but as the fly comes forward as it normally would on a roll cast, swiftly bring the rod to the rear the same as you would for a normal backcast. You'll get an acceleration of line speed and will easily be able to shoot ten or more feet of line on the forward cast with no false casting.

Another way to get acccelerated line speed is with a water haul. This cast is especially useful in windy conditions when you need to drive a fly directly into the wind or when you are casting heavily weighted stream-

Water Haul A.
The fly and line have just landed on the water. Take note of the low rod tip, which is necessary for a quick line pickup.

Water Haul B. Immediately after the fly and line land on the water, briskly lift the rod while yanking down with the line hand. This is an excellent way to get greatly increased line speed when casting long distances or into the wind.

ers long distances. A water haul in either case will allow you to cast far greater distances without making several false casts to extend line. Cast as far as you comfortably can and allow the forward cast to land on the water.

Immediately lower the rod tip to the water's surface and strip in any loose line with your line hand at the same time. Then abruptly raise the rod to the backcast position while yanking the line with your line hand, and allow some line to shoot to the rear.

Briskly bring the rod forward while giving the line a yank with your line hand. You'll be able to shoot a fourteen-inch or smaller loop for greater distance simply because the surface drag on your fly and line as you pick it up will generate a great deal of line speed. It's basically a double haul that is executed after one of the forward casts lands briefly on the water. Once again, it's a little noisy and requires a little extra strength and good timing. If you do a lot of big water fishing, you should practice this one until it consistently works for you.

Sometimes you simply must be on the wrong side of the stream. It's a position where the stream is on your left and the bank is on your right (for right-handers). You want to cast upstream, but there are bushes that won't allow a normal over-the-shoulder cast. I try to solve this by facing the center of the stream and casting the fly downstream, then reversing the line direction to present the fly upstream. It amounts to a cross-body cast. You'll probably not be as accurate as you'd like, but with a little practice you can make it work.

Depending on the length of the cast, I always try to keep all the retrieved line in small loops in the palm of my line hand but never wrapped around my thumb and fingers. It's a simple matter to make a loop over your thumb and little finger and transfer each succeeding loop into the palm of your hand by sliding your thumb and fingers out of the loop and folding it down to your palm with your first and second fingers. This creates three- to four-inch loops piled on top of each other. Then,

Sometimes you're on the wrong side of the stream.
Use the cross-body cast to present your fly to a likely area.

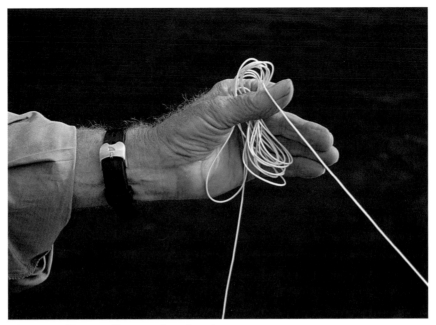

Close-up of loops of line in a hand retrieve.

when you go to shoot a little line, the coils will whisper from your hand much like spinning line from a reel. Like all things, it requires a little practice but will soon become an automatic reflex. You'll be amazed at how much line you can shoot on the forward cast with only one backcast.

There is a cast I learned from my old friend Koke Winter, the master of weird casts. It comes in handy when you're fishing large, fast rivers where the fish are also large and fast. I'm thinking of places like the Madison and Yellowstone rivers outside of Yellowstone National Park. On these rivers you must often cast across stream forty to sixty feet or more and land the fly on the far side of a series of variable speed currents. Immediately after the fly lands on the water, quickly strip (or have ready) five or six feet of line from the reel, lift the rod tip slightly to one side, and instantly throw a tight roll cast directly toward the fly. It's rather a savage action. You will usually throw a small loop of line near the fly, and that is often just enough line to increase a drag-free drift by as much as three or four feet.

It's also possible to throw this smaller loop nearly anyplace between you and the fly to increase the length of a drag-free drift. Just make sure the loop falls to the upstream side of your fly line.

Throw a small upstream loop near the fly on the far side of the stream to increase the length of a drag-free drift.

Throw a small upstream loop in midstream to compensate for a faster current crease in the middle of the river.

This one really feels good when it works, especially when a big fish takes the fly just before it begins to drag across current. (The described action is much like throwing a loop against the far bank or behind your fly to dislodge it from an exposed tree root or rock. Briskly raise your rod the moment the loop lands behind the fly. The sudden tug in the opposite direction will often free your fly.) Be ready to set the hook when you try this one, because the action of the tight roll cast will often cause the fly to twitch as much as six or eight inches and can trigger a strike when you least expect it.

Another time to use this cast is when you are fishing a large river and need to get your fly under a tree that's too low to the water for any kind of normal cast. It's a variation of a tight roll cast and the roll cast you would use to retrieve a fly stuck in the far bank. Cast the fly to land just short of the target. Then make a tight roll cast with your rod out to your side two or three feet above the water, and throw a fierce forward roll to create a loop no more than two or three feet high. The shallow loop will throw the fly back under the branches. It's not pretty to watch but can be most effective. There will be a little noise as you rip the line off the water and shoot the loop forward. A lot of my casting might not be pretty, but I don't really give a damn what others might think of what I'm doing with the rod and line. I'm only concerned with getting the fly to land where I want it to go and where it goes after it hits the water. This is a good cast when there is just enough wind to screw up your regular cast.

Winds, breezes, and air gusts can really screw up an otherwise fine cast. The worst challenge is trying to cast directly into the wind. The best advice I can give if you must cast into the wind is to keep your body and

After the fly has landed on the water, throw a tight roll cast to put the fly way back under the brush.

Low-profile power casting to drive the fly under the wind.

rod as low to the water as possible and work to gain the tightest loop and fastest line speed you can muster. Kneel if you can (or crouch as low as you are able), and keep your rod as parallel to the surface as possible. The wind speed near the water's surface is usually a little less than it is five or six feet above it.

Breezes and tiny gusts of air will often create a cushion of air near the far bank or next to a boulder or log. Try to think of air currents as an activity like stream currents and use them to your advantage. This may mean that you will have to present your fly far away from where the air and stream currents will push it. Since you can't see air currents, you're going to have to experiment with fly placement, casting speed, and target selection. When you get them all right, your fly will end up where you want it. Steady breezes are a little more time-consuming to figure out. You will have to make several casts against the bankside to figure out how much air is bouncing back at you. A right shoulder breeze will suddenly blow your fly and six feet of leader to your left simply because the air speed next to the bank seems to increase as it bounces off the bank in what amounts to a sudden change of direction. A left shoulder breeze will do just the opposite. Air puffs are those little gusts of breeze that come and go and are a little easier to deal with. All you have to do is be patient, wait until the gust has passed, and then make your cast. It's another instance when timing is everything. It's also another situation when the accuracy of your cast is important because your opportunities for presenting the fly are restricted.

There is another variation to the roll cast that I often use when I find myself in a position where I can't roll-cast as far as I need to, and even if I could, the large loop at the end of the cast would hang the fly in some low tree branches that always seem to be guarding one of the best holding spots. You just know there's a big fish back under those branches! The problem is that there are just enough tall bushes and trees behind you that a backcast is out of the question, and you can't wade any deeper. In a situation like this, I roll-cast as far as I can just to get some line out. Then I strip out enough line to put the fly where I want, allowing the roll cast to flow directly downstream with the additional line. When all the line has straightened, lower the rod tip to the surface and lift it with great force while yanking down firmly with the line hand. Stop the rod straight up, and then drift back slightly. About midway through the backcast, begin the forward cast while sharply applying wrist pressure. Roll the rod to a 45-degree angle to the upstream side and firmly power the remainder of the cast with your thumb, making certain that the thumb points directly at your target. The rod will travel in what amounts to a position from 12:00 to either 2:30 or 10:30, depending on whether the stream is flowing to your left or your right. It's a good cast for whacking yourself in the back of the neck with the fly as you finish! When it's done right, the fly will come whizzing past your ear just over your head. This one definitely takes some practice and perfect timing. Like most things in fly casting, it feels pretty good when it works.

Long line downstream ready to pick up. Notice that the rod tip is low to the water and the line hand is in a position to yank on the line.

Position of rod after the brisk pickup and line hand yank.

Stop rod straight up and drift back slightly.

The forward cast with upstream reach.

One of my favorite casts in tight situations is what I call an air mend to the roll cast. It's very similar to the cast just described, but it is executed over a much shorter distance. Allow the fly to drift downstream, execute the roll cast as described previously, but apply an upstream mend to the line before anything lands on the water.

Rod in position for a roll cast.

The forward roll.

The added air mend.

So much for the stiff wrist. It might sound blasphemous, but I don't think I could cast for two minutes without bending my wrist. I lift the line with a stiff arm and wrist, and as the line begins to come toward me, I increase the line speed with my wrist snapping to the rear and stop the rod at a 12:00 to 1:00 position. I begin my forward cast with a stiff arm and wrist, and as the line begins to come forward, I apply wrist pressure to tighten the loop, stopping the rod at an 11:00 position, pointing my rod tip at the fly, and following it down to the surface. To tighten the loop even more, I follow the wrist snap on the forward cast with added thumb pressure and a slight tug on the line with my line hand. I've found that if I try to keep my wrist from bending, I end up with a line loop that is about six feet high, and it all unrolls on the water, not in the air!

Most of my casting is done with wrist action only when I'm fishing tiny little mountain streams with lots of brush on both sides. It's a great way to tighten the loop down to a little more than a foot, and it increases accuracy to within an inch or two.

The worst thing you can do when casting is to allow your wrist to open on the backcast. By an open wrist, I mean that the palm of your hand is facing away from you.

This is an excellent way to ruin any kind of rod because each cast is twisting all the fibers. I can't imagine how you could make an accurate fly presentation. A good way to prevent an open wrist on the backcast is to concentrate on keeping your thumb in line with the cork grip and imagine you're hammering a nail that's nose high.

I learned to fly-fish on small streams in Michigan where the streambank always seemed to be lined with alders that were six to eight feet tall.

An open wrist on the backcast is a good way to ruin any fly rod.

A good example of a high backcast.

A low forward cast will increase your accuracy.

I think that's a good thought to keep in mind. Make every cast as if there are eight-foot-tall bushes behind you. You'll develop greater line speed, loop control, and accuracy if the backcast is higher than your head. The other thing I try to remember is to make the forward cast unroll no more than three or four feet above the water. Again, it's casting accuracy that counts in almost every case, and this forward cast will help loads.

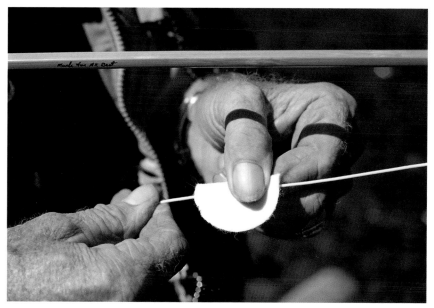

Clean your line several times a day.

You'll be able to cast better if your floating fly line is absolutely clean and, if the manufacturer recommends it, slightly lubricated with a product they produce. You must be able to lift the line from the water with as little water drag as possible. Not many of the casts I've described will work with a dirty line that clings to the surface. Clean your line every three or four hours of fishing. You'll be surprised how much grime a line can collect even when you're fishing crystal clear streams. In a pinch, you can use a good quality paste fly floatant to clean your line.

You must have a rod that is powerful enough to handle the water you intend to fish. Large rivers usually hold large fish. On big rivers 3- and 4-weight rods just don't work. You'll be unnecessarily stressing both the rod and the fish. I seldom use a rod less than 8½ feet in length and rarely use a line as light as a DT 4 F. My greatest joy in fly fishing is to fool the fish with the fly I present. If I or the fish misses the strike, so be it; I fooled the fish into striking. When I hook up a fish, I want to land it and put it back as soon as possible. If you get the opportunity to fish large rivers, you need to be able to muscle large fish. Light rods just won't let you do that. I'd strongly suggest an 8-foot 6-inch rod for a 6-weight line as a minimum for fishing large rivers. Much of the casting I've described can't happen with light lines.

The most important thing to remember in any casting situation is that the forward section of fly line and leader loop will determine how you present the fly. Your fly will always go in the same direction as this forward loop. The total length of the loop includes your leader and about six or eight feet of line. The rest of the fly line between your rod tip and the forward loop is merely a connection between you and the loop. Get control of the loop, lengthen line, and direct it to aim the loop. Line speed controls the height of the loop. The faster the line is going, the smaller (or tighter) the loop.

I have typically used a 7½-foot 4- or 5-weight rod when fishing the small 4- to 8-foot-wide streams that trickle down out of the mountains. Lately I find myself choosing heavier line rods that will work more efficiently for me when I need them to.

The forward loop will determine the direction of the fly.

Presentation begins when the fly hits the water, continues throughout the entire drift, and ends when the fly is picked up for the next cast. The fly must sit on the water so that it appears as if it's not attached to anything. I like to use the heaviest tippet I can get away with to accomplish that. There is a formula that goes back several decades to determine tippet diameter in relation to the fly size. I think it's fly size divided by three. If you are fishing a size 18 dry fly you're supposed to use 6X tippet. Don't do it! There are dozens of variables in every fly-fishing situation that will nullify any kind of rule about the ratio of tippet to fly size. An important one is water clarity. The best way to choose tippet strength is to watch the naturals a little and notice how they are floating downstream. Cast your fly next to a natural to see how it compares. If the natural appears to be alive and your fly is floating a little heavier, your tippet is too stiff. Presentation is more than getting a simple drag-free float. And you need to consider the size of the fish you are after.

Dry-fly presentation can involve a couple of tricks. One I discovered while I was fishing a stretch of water on the South Platte River in Colorado. The river came from my left side and got squeezed against the far bank by a slight curve upstream. The channel varied in depth from two to four feet and had a nice current crease on my side and also twelve inches of quiet water tight against the far bank. A chain link fence anchored with L-shaped steel posts to keep animals from getting away was part in the water and part out. The last steel post stood by itself, with no chain link section, and no more than two inches behind it was a very nice trout that ate every blue-winged olive that got caught in the tiny patch of dead water behind the post. Casting to the water was useless because every time the fly landed in that little four-inch circle, the cross-currents ripped it away before the trout had a chance to eat it. I fished to that trout for three days before I finally was able to cast a fly on a piled tippet that dribbled down the downstream side of the post and bobbed three times before the trout ate it. It's what I call a three-bob float. If you can get your fly to bob three times in a tough spot, you'll probably get a strike.

A pile cast is simply an underpowered open-loop cast that allows the tippet to fall to the water in a small pile. It's an important cast to learn, but you have to be careful setting the hook so that you don't overpower the strike and snap the fly off.

It's possible to achieve what appears to be a perfect drag-free float. But if your fly doesn't follow the tiny current creases that occur in every stream, you won't get a strike. All your fly has to do to alarm your quarry

The pile cast. Notice the white fly a little higher than my head in front of the bushes.

is drift across one of those tiny current creases, and it will be refused. Sometimes all it takes is an inch or two of cross-current drift, but the trout will notice something is wrong. To correct, simply take a step or two to the left or right before you make the next cast. Be aware of the speed of the surface current and your fly. You'll have drag if both aren't a perfect match. I've found that the best way for me to achieve a drag-free float is to present my cast in a direction that is across and slightly downstream. That is to say, if the stream is running from 12:00 to 6:00, I'll stand in a position that allows me to present the cast at an 8:00 or 4:00 angle, depending on whether upstream is to my right or left. The fly will always come to the trout before any leader, and if I present the cast lightly, there is very little line splash to alarm the fish. Occasionally, it's a good idea to give the fly a slight tug at the end of the drift to sink it and then execute a slow, hand-twist retrieve as you guide the fly across the currents with the rod. There will be times when this aggravates another trout into striking. The other added effect is that you won't spook your target fish by ripping line off the water in your hurry to make the next cast.

I know a couple of folks who pride themselves on fishing with nothing but 2-weight rods and 7X tippet. They are either fishing for small trout in small streams or making a horrible confession. I always figure that if the *average* size trout in a stream is twelve inches, that must mean there are some that are significantly larger, and sooner or later I'll hook up with one. I want a rod that can handle an 18-inch fish with no harm to the fish or the rod. Sometimes we are limited in the size of fish we can land simply because a 7X tippet is mandatory if we expect anything to eat a size 22 or 24 dry fly. Those are just the breaks. We're not ever going to be able to land all the big ones, but you can always walk away knowing that you fooled one!

Most of what I've written about has to do with fishing the dry fly, which I prefer over any other type of fly fishing. There are, however, ways to fool trout that involve subsurface flies. When the term subsurface is mentioned, most people think of nymphs. Nymph fishing has become popular among fly fishers whose only goal is to catch fish. I don't particularly enjoy nymph fishing because I'm not very good at it and will only resort to it when I haven't seen a rise in several hours. But when I do fish nymphs, I prefer not to use strike indicators because I think they look too much like bobbers. I think fishing with a bobber insults the fish. And we all credit fish with a lot more intelligence than they really have! I prefer to fish one nymph at a time. Trying to cast two flies with some weight on the tippet above them isn't pretty to watch, even when it's done right. I usually end up with a hell of a tangle, something like a spider web that's been caught up in a whirlwind. All I need to see is one rise and I'll switch to a dry fly immediately! And speaking of tangles, don't get upset when you find you've wrapped your body, neck, or arm with loops of fly line and tippet. It happens to us all, and it's usually after we've missed a strike. The best thing to do is to get control of where the fly is going by throwing a sharp roll cast in the air to your right or left. You must keep your line, leader, and fly in midstream. Regain line speed, loop control, and direction, and make another presentation. If your buddy snickers at your dilemma, it's because he totally understands and is happy to see it happen to someone else. I've been fly fishing for almost forty years now, and it still happens to me now and then. It's just part of the game. If anyone tells you that it never happens to him, he's lying!

**Oh, man.
I missed a good one.**

For shallow water nymph fishing (say two feet or less), I'll use a big buoyant dry fly such as a hopper or Wulff pattern to which I'll tie the required amount of tippet to the bend of the hook and then attach the nymph with just enough lead-substitute putty a few inches above the nymph to get it to within a few inches of the bottom.

My favorite way to rig a dry and a nymph dropper.

Greased leader butt coils provide the most sensitive strike indicator when nymph fishing.

For deeper water, I prefer to watch the leader and line junction, which I grease with floatant. It's a very sensitive strike indicator. In fact, if you know you're going to do some deep water nymph fishing, don't straighten the last two feet of your leader butt. Liberally grease it with fly floatant, and it will float on the surface like an open slinky. It's the most sensitive strike indicator I know. In either case, you must cast the fly to land well above the spot where the trout may be holding in order to give the nymph time to sink.

Casting a nymph rig isn't too difficult as long as you remember to slow everything down. I do most of my nymphing with what is known as the high-stick style. I recommend using an 8½-foot rod (minimum length) and a 12-foot leader. You need to keep as much line and leader off the water as possible, which means that you must get quite close to your target. Use extreme stealth, and approach your target from below and to the side of the run. Get the nymph down to the fish's holding level quickly and try not to get hung up on rocks and debris that may be on the bottom. You may have to test the amount of weight you put on the tippet and how far above the nymph you place it. I begin by stripping enough line from the reel to expose two to three feet of fly line beyond the tip-top guide, and then I roll-cast downstream a couple of times to extend both leader and line to reach my target. Depending on the depth of the area you are going to nymph, you should aim your fly to land about four to five feet above the intended drift area. This will give the nymph and lead weight time to sink to the proper depth. I can't give you a formula for the distance to cast or the amount of weight to add to the tippet, since every run you fish will be at a different depth and speed. Trial and error is the best method to determine how it's going to go. After you've had some experience judging depth, current speed, nymph size, and weights, you'll be able to estimate how it all works. If you're not getting hung up on the bottom now and then, you probably aren't getting deep enough. If you are getting hung up on the bottom every cast, remove a tiny bit of weight from the leader. This is very easy to do if you use a lead-substitute putty.

High-stick nymph fishing with a bushy dry fly in the current crease and the nymph bouncing along the bottom immediately under the indicator.

Cast your nymph rig downstream until you think you have enough line out beyond the rod tip, and allow the current to straighten it out. Then with one sweeping overhand cast, fling the nymph rig to land upstream from the target. Follow the nymph and weight with your rod tip, which should be horizontal and near the water's surface when the nymph hits the water. As the current brings the fly and weight downstream, use your line hand to gather loose line as you raise the rod tip to keep as much line as possible off the water. Make every attempt to keep the leader perpendicular to the fly. This will prevent the drag of the current on your leader and line from sweeping your fly across the bottom currents. Should that happen, the trout will refuse your fly. Allow the current to straighten your leader and line as the fly drifts through the run. Then, lift and use a sweeping overhead cast to fish the run again. It may take several drifts in the same spot to get any action.

Try to cover every square inch of the bottom of the run you're fishing. Oftentimes, it's a good idea to switch to a smaller nymph if you're getting no takers. I usually figure that if a trout won't eat a small Gold-Ribbed Hare's Ear, a Pheasant Tail, or *Baetis* nymph, I'm probably wasting my time. However, before you give up on nymphing, try several other likely holding runs. You will occasionally find that trout aren't feeding in one run, but ten feet away they'll gobble whatever you give them. That's what I love about fishing streams.

You'll have to employ some line-mending techniques (flipping some loose line upstream) to prevent the line on the surface from going faster than the nymph is drifting. Presentation in nymph fishing is just as important as in dry-fly fishing. And remember, presentation ends when you pick up the fly for the next cast. Don't forget to allow the current to raise your fly to the surface at the end of the drift. Trout will often take a nymph as it's rising. In fact, it's also a good idea to use your rod to guide the fly across the current for a few feet after it comes to the surface. You may get a strike as you fish the nymph in a wet-fly style, and you'll also be setting yourself up for the next presentation with a single forward cast.

Another good technique to use when fishing nymphs (or streamers) in very deep runs is to add enough weight to get the nymph down to the bottom as quickly as possible. Move to the head of the run and cast your rig upstream just far enough to get it to sink to the bottom at the head of the deep run. Strip a little line out while lifting the rod tip to bounce the rig downstream a few inches. Continue the walking action all the way down to the tailout, and then bring it back with a series of hand-twist retrieves and a slight rod-lifting action. If there's a hog down there, this is an excellent way to get it to eat your fly. You must use floating nymphs and streamers or you'll lose all your flies! The extra split shot or lead putty will get your fly down to very near the bottom where you want it, but the flotation built into your fly will prevent it from going into the rocks. Unweighted Muddlers and greased nymphs constructed of hollow hair are the secret to this technique.

For those times when nymphing just doesn't produce, I dig in my vest for the little fly box that contains a dozen or more streamers. There are weighted black and olive Wooly Buggers, weighted gold Muddlers, sparsely tied Black-Nose Dace, Clouser Mickey Finns, weighted dark and light Spruce flies, and a couple of weighted yellow marabou Spruce fly streamers. All in sizes 6 and 8. I usually try to fish with 5X tippet when nymphing, but, when I go to streamers, I'll always retie my leader with two feet of 4X tippet. I resist tying a weighted streamer onto a 5X tippet, simply because it's there. I can't begin to tell you how many streamers I have snapped off on the backcast or lost on a surprisingly large fish while using 5X. Take the time to clip your leader back to 3X and add the proper tippet. On large rivers, I'd suggest going down to 3X tippet. Trust me, you'll be glad you did.

Fishing streamers involves a little of what I call kamikaze fishing. The fish you're after is usually in some kind of secure cover, under a log, deep behind or in front of a boulder, or in an undercut bank full of roots. You must get your streamer down deep enough or back in far enough so that whatever is hiding in there can't resist eating it. You are going to get hung up now and then and lose a streamer or two, but that's part of the price you have to pay. If you're lucky enough to hook one of these big boys, the 3 or 4X will give you a little advantage in muscling it out into the current where you can play it and land it.

Weighted streamers are a must if you expect to have any success in drawing the big trout out to eat your fly. I always try to put myself in a casting position that is above and to the side of my target area. This will allow me to place the fly within a few inches of the far bank (in the case of undercuts), and with a little line stripping and mending, I can usually achieve a long enough drift to either get snagged on some underwater roots or branches or get a strike. I've mentioned line mending several times, but perhaps the term "line tending" is more accurate. You must tend to the line between your fly and rod at all times, no matter what kind of fly you're fishing. When I'm streamer fishing, I like to extend the drift by keeping the line in a current crease. Sometimes I will flip a small loop into a faster current, which will cause the streamer to swim across the current just in front of a boulder when the stream pulls the loop down to the fly. Then I'll throw another loop in the opposite direction to make the streamer swim across in the other direction. This can be a deadly technique. Just remember, a streamer is only effective when it's in the water.

Always fish out the cast when you're fishing streamers. Use your rod to guide the fly around in front of and behind every possible lie in the stream. If the stream is small enough, you'll be able to fish most of both sides. Use your rod tip or line hand to make the fly dance around the obstacles. You want to make your streamer appear to be alive. Sometimes it's a good technique to make the streamer dart a foot or two as it crosses the currents to give the appearance of something that's trying to escape.

Throwing a loop of line across the stream to pull the streamer to other likely holding areas.

I like to use a WF floating line on larger rivers and will stay with a DT floating line on smaller streams. To make sink tips instantly, I do carry some short lengths of lead-core trolling line on a small spool in my vest. You can make up some of these by whipping a loop in each end of a 3-, 4-, and 5-foot length of lead-core line. They're not much fun to cast, but they are effective. You'll be glad you had them on hand when you're a mile from your truck and you have just found a six-foot-deep hole that you know holds a big fish. Cut your leader back to 0X, tie a double overhand knot to create a loop in the leader butt, and loop the lead core to it. Then tie a double overhand knot in a two-foot length of 2X, and loop connect it to the lead core. The 2X will be your tippet and will break off before you lose the whole rig should you get snagged on a sunken log or rock.

Streamer fishing is best done with a rod that is at least 8½ feet long and designed to throw a DT 6 F line. A 9-foot rod is better. If I think I might be streamer fishing, I'll stick a spool of WF 7 F line in my vest. The weight-forward line makes casting a weighted streamer long distances a whole lot easier.

6

Flies

You can be a better-than-average caster, do everything right, and eliminate most all the complications to your day of fishing, but if you don't have the correct fly tied to your tippet, you will have a frustrating time.

I've encouraged you to examine spider webs and check out the little stillwater back eddies and shore lines. And all this will provide you with important information. But it's far better to know what's been hatching during the few days prior to your time on the water. I think trout do get accustomed to certain foods and their availability. Sometimes it pays to arrive before the hatch begins and fish the water by casting your fly to likely holding water. You must be careful when you do this because you can spook an entire run if your presentations and pickups are splashy. If you've been sloppy and spooked the fish, then when the hatch does begin, there will be no rising fish. If you don't get a few strikes with this technique within a few minutes, it might be a good idea to go sit on the bank and wait for the hatch to begin.

If you are fishing some familiar water, you probably already know what the calendar suggests. But since Mother Nature has a nasty habit of changing things a bit to suit her needs, it is well worth the few bucks it costs to make some phone calls to local fly shops and ask what insects they are seeing. It's an even better idea to stop in on your way to the water and buy a couple of flies. Many of the fly shops will have a hatch board posted with the information you need for fishing local streams and lakes. The trouble is it's usually yesterday's information! In the end, you're going to have to make a semieducated guess about what fly to tie on first. There are some really good shops with websites that provide most of the information you need. All you have to do is negotiate through the myriad headings to find what you want, and the information is free. Although these websites are primarily designed to sell products, the good ones also provide valuable information on the fishing in the area plus the merchandise they have in stock or, better yet, on sale.

Indulge me, please, while I rant a bit about buying flies. If you have already spent hundreds or thousands of dollars on rods, reels, line, waders, vest, net, rain gear, polarized glasses, and a vehicle to get to the stream, are you one of those who balks at paying two bucks for a fly? And are you one of those who screams about the poor quality of foreign-tied flies that cost $12.00 a dozen? Do you wonder why we can't get more flies tied in the United States? Too many of us want to buy flies at wholesale prices. The tier wants to make a modest profit and cover his expenses, which include the cost of materials and taxes (both income and excise), and some operating expenses like water, heat, and light. Your local fly shop is trying to support U.S. tiers and make a profit as well. I'd say if you can buy flies tied in the United States for $3.00 each, it's a damn good deal. After all, the fly is something you can't do without!

If there's a hatch on when you arrive and trout are rising, solving the problem of what fly to use just got easier. Net a bug, find a fly in your box that matches, and tie it on. Sounds simple enough, but of course, it doesn't always work. I usually begin with a matching dun pattern. If the dun doesn't bring any strikes, I'll switch to a parachute version of the same pattern. And if that doesn't work, I'll tie on a quill-body spinner that matches the species. The spinner almost always brings up some trout. Sometimes none of what I've suggested is effective. It's then that I will go down to a floating emerger pattern, and if that doesn't work, I'll tie on a greased floating nymph.

Then there are those tantalizing days when there is a multiple hatch. I've seen it many times on the Frying Pan and South Platte rivers in Colorado. The Frying Pan is famous for hatches of PMDs, BWOs, saratellas, midges, green drakes, *flavilineas,* and a few sulphurs coming off at the same time! Toss in a couple of color variations of some caddis, and the trout have a smorgasbord to choose from. It feels real good when you finally find the pattern a trout is hungry for. Trouble is, the next trout three feet away is probably feeding on something different, and you have to go through another dozen fly changes to find out what that might be. It always pays to have an extra spool of tippet when fishing the Pan. There will be days when nothing you do by way of fly changes will solve the problem. What to do? Terrestrials such as hoppers, red or black ants, and small bronze- or black-winged beetles will often save an otherwise frustrating day.

Then there are the days when we are completely humiliated. There are rising trout in every place they should be. We can see the flies on the water, even watch them disappear as trout of all sizes gobble them. We go to finer and longer tippets and change flies a dozen times, yet not one fish will come to our flies. We check size and color every few casts, change our casting position from time to time, make sure we have a perfect drag-free float, but still we can't get one dink to eat our fly. It does happen.

I vividly remember fishing with Roy Palm (the guru of the Pan and owner of Frying Pan Anglers Fly Shop) one afternoon during a heavy hatch of PMDs. Dozens of trout were eagerly taking duns from the surface within twelve to fifteen feet of us. There we were with nearly a hundred years of collective fly-fishing experience and couldn't catch even one little 10-incher! We each used up two or three 30-inch tippets in fly changes trying to figure out what the hell the trout wanted. We never got it right and left the stream after nearly two hours of casting with nary a refusal rise! We agreed that it was a good thing that no one witnessed our being so totally humbled.

I'm an admitted hatch matcher, but I do always carry a selection of Adams duns and parachutes in sizes 12 through 18 and some Royal Wulffs in sizes 8 through 18. There are some brawling streams not far away that I like to visit now and then, and these heavily hackled flies are easy to see and tend to float a little longer before they get drowned. Usually it's just long enough for some trout to see the fly and strike. These are great flies to use when you decide to fish the heavy water that no one else does. The Adams is almost a generic hatch matcher in any size, and the Royal Wulff is one of the most effective attractor patterns ever devised.

My favorite mayfly patterns are stripped and dyed quill bodies in sizes 26 through 16. I use dyed wild turkey biots for flies size 14 and larger. I tie all my duns, parachutes, and spinners with only those two body materials. I make my quills from six- to eight-inch-long strung Chinese rooster neck hackle. Don't use saddle hackle; the quills are too small in diameter. Four- to six-inch-long Chinese rooster neck hackle is available, but the longer feathers I use have larger diameters that more accurately match the segmentation width on the body of most mayflies up to size 16. I think I've tried just about every kind of natural material that's available to match the light-reflective, waxy appearance of a natural mayfly. I've had my best success with stripped and dyed quills and find them easiest to tie with. The reason, I think, is the feather quill is not hollow but is filled with a pithlike substance that prevents it from flattening when wrapped around the hook shank. With a variety of diameters you can tie flies all the way down to size 26 and still match the segmentation widths of the naturals, and when you apply a good quality silicone-base waterproofing agent, the flies float like little corks.

There seems to be some confusion about the fragility of a quill-body fly, which I think is based on flies such as the Quill Gordon. The Quill Gordon body is made not from a quill but from a stripped peacock herl. The quill of a peacock feather is the center stem. But since it's called a *Quill* Gordon and the body is fragile, we assume all quill-body flies are fragile and need to be reinforced in some way. Not so! I don't counterwrap with fine wire nor do I apply a thin coat of any kind of lacquer to any of my quill-body flies. I have some quill-body flies in my fly boxes that I have fished for three years, and they're as solid as the day I tied them.

The idea of using stripped and dyed quills came to me about twenty years ago when John Gierach and I were fishing a blue-winged olive hatch with the standard, dubbed-body Blue-Winged Olive pattern. We were on a famous stretch of the South Platte River in Colorado, and both of us were getting far too many refusals. I resorted to my usual practice of netting the naturals in a little aquarium net and comparing them with my dubbed-body dry fly. It was a moment of epiphany. I had the right-size fly, the wings were the right height, and the colors matched perfectly, but the bodies of the naturals weren't fuzzy! They were prominently segmented and waxy in appearance. Do this and you'll discover that no mayfly has a fuzzy body.

I've read that certain dubbing materials give a translucency to the body of mayfly patterns. Translucency means light is passing through, but light does not pass through a mayfly dun. It is reflected *from* their bodies. The female spinner does look somewhat translucent after she has deposited her eggs. I'm of the opinion that a dubbed body on a spinner is far too large in diameter to accurately match the natural but the stripped and dyed quill is the perfect material for most spinners and duns since it presents a slim, well-segmented body.

The reason I use dyed wild turkey biots on flies larger than size 16 is simply because it's very difficult to find feathers whose quills are large enough to match the segmentation of flies at that size. Wild turkey biots are waxy in appearance, reflect light, provide prominent segmentation markings, and are long enough to create the body of a mayfly if you're tying on a size 12 long shank hook. The only problem with wild turkey biots is that even though they do get wider toward the bases, they do not get appreciably thicker. Building a gradual taper to the body is very difficult unless you apply some fine dubbing from the thorax area to near the tail before you tie the biot onto the hook. You can accomplish this easily if you dub size 14 body on a size 12 hook, beginning at the thorax and tapering toward the hook bend. Save just enough room between the end of the body and the tailing material to tie in the tip of the biot.

Nearly all the mayfly dun patterns I see in fly shops around the country are tied following the old proportion chart recommendations. I wish that piece of information had never been written. The tail lengths and wing heights of every mayfly species I have seen are either longer or shorter or taller than the proportion charts dictate. Colorado's green drake has a tail that is half its body length and a wing height equal to the length of the entire body, from the tip of its nose to the end of its tails. The Trico dun has very short tails and wings about a size too big, both in height and in width. Some size 18 blue-winged olives have wings that belong on a size 16 hook. If you tie your own flies, please throw away the damn proportion chart and start taking photos of the naturals in your stream. The camera doesn't lie and is, in fact, a wonderful teacher. If you tie your own flies, you always begin with a bare hook, so why not build everything into your flies that matches the naturals as closely as you can? Study the natural's proportions, colors, and body. There are no unimportant details, but I warn you to be careful that you don't go over the edge. There is a limit to how much detail and work you want to put into your flies. I aim for accurate imitation, but I don't want to feel like shooting myself if I lose a fly.

John Gierach once said that it occurred to him that he was never going to be able to catch all the trout. It has been made painfully clear to me that there are days when I am not going to catch any trout. And that's what keeps me going back.

7

Setting the Hook

Setting the hook when dry-fly fishing is pretty much an instinctive reflex action. But you have to be paying close attention to how the fish has taken your fly. Sometimes, especially when you're fishing a dry caddis imitation, the trout will almost set the hook on the take because its strike is rather explosive. All you have to do is tighten the line. "All you have to do is tighten the line" is the key phrase here. The trout's take is often so surprising that I have sometimes overreacted and launched some little 4-incher over my shoulder! That's when I pray no one was watching. Those little 4-inchers can sometimes eat a fly with more gusto than a 14-incher. And, I must admit, I've snapped the fly off in the jaws of a large trout by setting up too hard. Then again, when I'm fishing a spinner fall at dusk, I'll casually raise the rod tip on what seemed like an insignificant rise only to find that I've hooked a 20-incher that inhaled my little Red Quill spinner with hardly a dimple in the surface. Sometimes you get to see the trout's face as it comes up to eat your dun. Other times, you see only a small whirlpool where the fly once was, and that can indicate that a large trout just ate your fly. No two trout seem to feed the same way. You have to spend countless hours on the stream to know what to do, and even then, you're going to be surprised now and then.

Always watch a rising trout for a few minutes before making your first cast. Try to determine if the trout is holding in one spot and simply rocking up and down to sip flies or drifting back with the fly and rising two or sometimes even three feet below its holding spot. You will sometimes see a trout move forward to intercept the fly. Watch the insects that float near the trout. Does the fish move from side to side to feed or does it wait for something to come directly over its nose? You will also discover the trout's feeding style. Sometimes brown trout like to feed in what appears to be a vertical position with their heads coming straight up out of the water. Was that a small whirlpool, an audible sucking sound, or just a dimple on the surface? The few moments you spend making these observations will greatly increase your chances of hooking up on the first fish take to your fly.

You need nerves of steel when you see a large fish rising out of the depths with its mouth open, ready to eat your fly. There have been many times when I have managed to save my fly just in the nick of time as I set up at the very moment the trout began to close its mouth. I always feel pretty dumb when this happens. But then, after a moment, I think, "You know, when you get so damn cool that you no longer do that, maybe it'll be time to quit fishing."

When you miss a fish, it's only natural to want to cast right back to the same spot in hopes that you won't miss again on the next strike. But, the trout will seldom make the same mistake twice. After I've missed a fish, I hardly ever get a strike on the very next cast. Brookies maybe and an occasional rainbow who's really on the feed, but brown trout seem to sulk down out of sight while they think it over. Rest the fish awhile; chances are it will begin feeding again in a few minutes.

There are times when you want to employ a slip strike. A slip strike can be done two ways. The most common way is to lift the rod tip *without* holding the line in your line hand. The action of the rod rising up coupled with the friction of the snake guides on the fly line will cause the line to move toward you slightly, firmly setting the hook and automatically allowing some slack line. It's a great technique to use when fishing very long and very fine tippets. I learned it years ago while fishing the chaff hatch on the north branch of Michigan's Au Sable River. Trout loved to sip a true size 28 cream-colored mayfly. Tippet sizes back in the 60s were far too big in diameter, so I was using monofilament sewing thread. I think it was 8X and tested a little less than one pound in strength. The only hope I had of setting up on a fish and not losing the fly was to use this slip strike. When I could land a 14-incher with that kind of set up, I was about as happy as I could be.

The second type of slip strike is when you do not raise the rod tip but use your line hand to give the line a little tug. Your rod tip needs to be at the water's surface for this, and there should be no slack in the line. People who do a lot of fishing for bonefish and permit know all about this technique. If you miss the fish, the fly has only moved a few inches, and you haven't spooked anything. It's very effective for trout fishing as well, especially if you're fishing a large glassy pool covered with spinners. If you set up in the usual fashion by briskly raising your rod and miss the strike, the surface disturbance will spook the glassy pool for the next few hours. If you use the line-hand tug, you'll only spook the fish under your fly if you should miss. It's a good way to set the hook if your rod is pointed directly at the fish, but, it's also a good way to lose both the fly and the fish. The key to keeping both is to hold the line between your thumb and forefinger just firmly enough to move the line and keep your rod at a slight angle to the fly line. When the fish takes the fly, slide the line through your grip loosely so you don't snap the tippet on an already tight line. The inertia of the fly line will set the hook in most instances. This is an excellent technique to use when you're fishing wet flies for large cruisers in a pond, since these fish will sometimes take the fly on a sudden turn and snap your tippet as if it were thread if the line is taut.

Most of the time, you can set up on the fish at the strike. There are times when you need to hesitate a little. This is especially true when you're fishing an across-and-downstream drift. You need to give the trout time to close its mouth and lower its head. Another important time to hesitate is when you know you are presenting your fly to a large fish. The little fish seem to be so hungry that they'll close their mouths the very instant they take the fly. Bigger fish can be much more casual, and if you set up too quickly, you'll snatch the fly out of their mouths before they have a chance to close on it. In the case of setting up on a larger fish, I always use a little trick: saying my full name and then setting up. If you have more than four or five syllables in your name, that may take too much time. Try instead the phrase, one-one thousand.

Your chances of missing strikes increase exponentially with the length of your cast. The more line you have out on the water, the more slack line you'll have between you and your fly. Your fly cannot move until all the slack has been removed. It's a hard and fast rule and another excellent reason to always pay attention to what the line is doing while at the same time watching your fly. Keep the S curves to a minimum and never allow a loop of line to form between you and your fly. This is all part of the presentation and can get a little complicated in fast-moving water. I will often hold the line from my reel under the index finger of my rod hand, as I gradually raise the rod tip and use my line hand to pull up the slack at the same time. It's as close to complete line control as you can get. This works very well when fishing pocket water or in streams up to twenty or thirty feet wide, when you're casting upstream to a specific spot with only a four- to five-foot drift.

There are those days when the fish will make a fool of you. I've seen trout come up to my dry fly and bump it with the tops of their heads! This often happens in heavily fished, catch-and-release waters. It's as if the trout is saying, "I've seen this pattern before, and you're not fooling me!" When that happens, it's time to change flies, either to a smaller version of what you're using or to another pattern entirely. It's a good time to switch to a small terrestrial, no matter what's hatching. Size 20 or 22 red ants often work.

The visual aids you have for help when nymph fishing are a strike indicator, a greased leader and line junction, or the greased butt section of your leader that has not been straightened. If you see hesitation in any one of the three in its drift, that could be a strike. The hesitation can be slight, so you'll have to pay attention. There is no such thing as an insignificant hesitation in whatever you're using as a strike indicator. Oftentimes it's merely the lead weight on the tippet bouncing along near the bottom that causes the indicator to exhibit a tiny jiggle. Set up anyway, gently raising the rod tip a few inches. If it's not a fish, or if it is and you miss it, your fly is still near the bottom. If a trout has eaten your fly, it'll be solidly hooked. It's been my experience that when trout are feeding on nymphs, they aren't charging the flies. They simply open their mouths and ingest the flies. These are the subtlest of all strikes and every fiber of your mind and body must be ready to react or you'll miss most of them.

The strikes you get when fishing streamers are usually anything but subtle, unless, of course, you're casting upstream and bringing the streamer down barely ahead of the current. It can be a deadly technique that I use a lot when fishing for smallmouth bass in a stream. It also works for trout hanging around boulders and sunken logs. The strike is usually a slight pull on the line that you'll easily miss if you're not paying close attention.

My favorite method of fishing streamers is to cast across and slightly downstream. I try to get my streamer to land as close to an undercut bank as possible. These are favorite places where larger-than-average trout hang out. By casting across and slightly downstream, I can throw a slack loop upstream and extend the bankside drift by several feet. If you can keep your streamer within a foot or two of the bank, chances are the trout that's hiding there will charge out and eat it. These can be vicious strikes, and if you're not careful, you'll snap the fly off by setting up too hard. It's another time to hesitate slightly. Trout that come out of an undercut will often take your streamer in a slashing strike as they turn back toward the bank, in which case all you have to do is raise the rod tip. Fish out a bankside cast by allowing the current to sweep your fly toward the middle of the stream. Twitch the fly as it comes near other holding spots such as sunken boulders, current creases, or logs. You can cover a lot of water fishing streamers, and you should take advantage of all the water your streamer swims through.

Oftentimes it's a good idea to allow your fly to disappear back into the undercut just in case there's an old recluse hiding back in there. Present your fly several times in such places. The old recluse might need some teasing.

8

Playing the Fish

There are as many variables to playing a fish as there are to casting. My rule is to always try to land the fish as quickly as possible to reduce the stress on the fish. The size of the fish, the size of the fly, the strength of the tippet, the speed of the water, obstructions in the water, and luck, all will influence how fast you land the fish. When I'm lucky enough to hook into a 20-incher, I figure it's really a good day when I can bring it to net.

The most important thing you can do before you even make your first cast is to adjust the drag on your reel so that the line won't continue to run out or overrun the reel when you strip it out (or the fish does). This simple act should be part of your routine every time you string up your rod. Another good reason to have your drag set rather weakly is that a good fish, say one 14 inches or longer, will often make one last burst toward freedom just as you think you've got it whipped. If your drag is set too tight, the tippet will break during this sudden lunge. The stronger you set your drag, the more apt you are to break off fish. I've never been able to figure out why some makers of trout reels put in a drag system that can be set to "stun." (Saltwater fishing excepted here.) A big fish is going to go where it wants, and about all you can do is try to steer it away from snags. Unless you give the big fish its head, you'll break off every one you try to stop. The best thing you can do when you have hooked into a real monster is to point your rod directly at it with the drag set just tight enough to prevent an overrun when the fish suddenly stops or jumps. This big fish will continue to fight the pressure on its first run as long as it can feel it. It will usually run down into the next pool. Let it go. Chances are it will go to the bottom of the deepest part of this pool where it will sulk for a few moments while you figure out how you're going to win the battle.

The more line you have on the water, the more drag there will be, due to the water's resistance. It's difficult to manage large amounts of line on the water when you hook a good fish that goes ballistic. Then it's best to keep as much line as possible off the water by holding your rod as high as you can so that only the leader is dragging through the water. You can still apply some side pressure to such a fish by lowering your rod slightly to the right or left, as you notice it's heading for trouble. By all means get this fish on the reel as soon as you can. Loose loops of line trailing downstream are an invitation to disaster. There will be times when a fish may run toward you and the only way you can gain line control is to strip in line as fast as you can. Here's a good technique, though it may be humorous to watch. Use both your line hand and your mouth. Strip in as much line as you can with you line hand, grab it with your mouth (not your teeth!), and take another hold of the line near the stripping guide with your line hand. Place each loop of line between your lips in front of the previous loops, and make sure they don't overlap. Repeat until you get some kind of control and then get all that loose line on your reel as soon as possible. This will prevent having a huge loop of line flowing downstream and getting snagged on the only stick in sight. If the fish makes a sudden change of direction, you'll be able to release the line in your

Fly fisher with rod held high and pointed straight at a fast-running large fish.

Fly fisher with rod straight up, slightly bent, a couple of line loops in his lips, and reaching up to the stripping guide for more line.

mouth instantly. Sometimes it's a good idea to back up or move upstream or down as you strip in line in order to keep some tension on the fly. It's also a good technique for line control when lake or ocean fishing while wading. Stripping in large amounts of line can cause trouble when getting ready to make the next cast. If the loose loops are held between your lips, you can easily shoot line on both back and forward casts.

Jumpers are fun to watch, and I say any fish that jumps or takes out line is a good fish, no matter what its size. But those jumps can be the kiss of death if you aren't quick as lightning in your reaction. A big jumping fish will probably snap your 6 or 7X tippet when it hits the water, especially if the tippet is tight. You need nerves of steel to be able to remember to drop your rod tip the very instant the fish goes airborne. This will put some slack in the line and greatly reduce the chances of your losing the fly and the fish when it lands in a splash. Having said that, you can also haul on the fish and slam it back into the water if you're using the heavier tippets as you'd use when streamer fishing. You'll turn the fish's head and gain some small degree of control as the fight begins.

Once you get your fish in open water, always apply side pressure by holding your rod nearly parallel to the water's surface. The fish will tire

Fly fisher with dropped rod tip and loose line and a large leaping trout.

much more quickly if you exert side pressure instead of top pressure. A good fish can go to the bottom, and you won't be able to budge it with a high rod. Big brown trout, especially, seem to like to behave this way. But you can move it out of its sulk if you apply side pressure. And here is a little trick I learned when I did a lot of bass fishing: Rap on the rod butt when the fish is sulking on the bottom like a water-soaked log. Use a lighter or pair of hemostats to rap on the butt cap, and send vibrations down the line to the fly. That will often send the fish on another dash for freedom, so be ready to give him some line.

A big fish will often run rapidly downstream and hide behind a rock or large boulder, and you can feel your leader tippet rasping on its sharp edges. If you're in a position where you can't get the leader over the rock to your side of the stream, or you can't move downstream because the water is too deep, the boulders too large, or the canyon too steep, you may lose both the fish and your fly. Don't try to pressure a large fish (or even a medium-size fish) when you face these challenges. Instead, strip

Fly fisher with bent rod held high and slightly to one side, slamming a large jumping fish with a streamer in its mouth back into the water.

Fly fisher standing in slack water applying side pressure to a fish in the main current.

some line off your reel as you raise your rod as high as you can. Then strip off a little more line as you slowly lower your rod tip to the surface and allow the current to belly the line to the fish's side. Apply some pressure when the loop of line gets well below the fish. This gives the fish a new sense of where the pressure is coming from and will often get it to move to another place and perhaps set up a situation where you can get downstream. There's a good chance you're going to lose this fish, but if you can get the fish to change its holding and sulking lie, you have some chance of landing it. It's a gamble at best, but sometimes gamblers win!

Look for a spot out of the strong currents of the stream where you can land your fish. There is often a gravel or sand bar nearby or perhaps a back eddy. I've seen a lot of good fish lost during the final moment of the fight because the fly fisher didn't move out of the current to a place of slack water to land the fish. I recommend you use a wading staff. If you're standing in fast water while you're fighting your fish, you'll be trying to land it in fast water, which only increases your chances of losing it. The best place to fight any fish is to one side of the main current. You fooled the fish on its terms, now battle it on yours.

I learned to land fish with a landing net, but I don't normally use it on fish that are less than 10 inches. Since I always fish flies with their barbs pinched, it's a simple matter to run my left thumb and forefinger down the tippet to the fly and back it out without lifting the fish from the water. Larger fish are a different matter because they don't always want to lie still while I do this, so with large fish, I bring them to the net. Always try to bring the fish into the net headfirst. Place your net in the water, and as soon as the fish's head reaches and passes the net's frame, drop the rod tip, and let the fish swim into the net. Netting a fish from the rear is chancy because when a large fish feels the net against the rear half of its body, it'll often make a sudden lunge for freedom. Your instinctive response will be to try to scoop the fish into the net anyway, which usually throws the fish forward. The fish will often win this one. If you do net the fish from the rear, drop your rod tip the moment your net has billowed open behind the fish. The current will wash the fish back into your net.

Never allow anyone else to land your fish, unless you are paying big bucks for a guide. You made the cast, you fought the fish to the end, now it's your job to land it. You don't want to lose a fish or a friend. Don't count on a fishing buddy to net your fish because if something goes wrong, you'll both blame each other. Most guides know how to net a fish, but having said that, you must know what to do when the guide puts the net under the fish. Always drop your rod tip the instant the net is under your fish, allowing the fish to drop back into the net and make you and your guide very happy.

It doesn't happen often, but you'll occasionally have a fish on that simply won't fit into your net. Don't even try to make it happen or you'll lose the fish. Look for a shallow beach on a sand or gravel bar and lead the monster in using the butt section of your rod. If you try to do this with the tip section of rod, you'll probably snap it off. Forget all about those photos we've all seen of rods that are bent double. That's advertising plain and simple. If they break a rod shooting that ad, they have a half dozen more as backups. If your rod breaks, you're done for the day!

Have you ever hooked a big fish and had it go nose first into some thick weeds or moss? Those of you who have fished the Henry's Fork in Idaho or Poindexter Slough in Montana know all about this. You have a couple of options when this happens: 1, Apply steady pressure with your

Fly fisher beaching a very large trout by leading it onto a beach using the rod's butt section.

rod tip high in the hopes that the weeds aren't too thick and maybe they'll separate enough to let you bring the fish up; 2, use the loose line technique in the hope that the fish will think it's free and swim out by itself; or 3, move downstream from your fish and apply steady pressure straight back over its head in an attempt to back it out. Option 3 is the last resort. Most of the time, you're going to lose the fish, and about all you can say is, "Well, I fooled it."

Many good fish are lost during the last few seconds of the fight. You want to land the fish after a long battle because you don't want to harm the fish any more than necessary. But if you try to hurry the last thirty seconds of a long fight, chances are you're going to lose the fish of the day. Take as much care and time as you did at the beginning of the fight. Normally I wait until I can get the fish's head up to the surface and keep it there before I try to lead it to the net.

9

Releasing the Fish

The goal is to land a fish as quickly as you can so that it will recover sooner from the fight. But removing the hook while the fish is still fresh might be a challenge. It's a lot easier to control a spunky fish when it's in the net. And in the interest of releasing a fish that's not totally worn out, use barbless hooks because they're easier to take out of the fish's mouth. Always remove the hook while your fish is still in the net, allowing the fish to stay in the water while you slide the hook out of its jaw. Try to turn the fish upside down before you remove the hook. Most trout will calm down when they're belly up and removing the hook will go a lot faster for you.

I can't fathom any reason why some people still want to fish with barbed fly hooks. The flies come out of my hat, shirt, neck, and fingers a hell of a lot easier when the barbs have been pinched down, and you'll avoid the embarrassment of having to go to the emergency room to have a hook removed. It takes more time to remove a barbed fly from a trout's mouth, and I don't want to spend any more time than I have to removing the same fly from a trout that I hope I can enjoy catching again. Many of the folks who say they prefer using flies with barbed hooks are catch-and-release fly fishers. But if you're going to release the fish, what does it matter if the fish happens to get away before you actually land it? I do lose a fish now and then when I fish barbless hooks, but most of those losses are due to a poorly tied knot, a broken tippet, or operator error.

Our goal in fly fishing is to have a fish eat the fly. To play and bring to net a large trout that you stalked and finally fooled is exciting. When a big one gets away it does leave me with a little touch of an empty feeling. But shouldn't the trout win sometimes? I have a friend who cuts the bend off his flies and counts his day's success in the number of takes he gets. I admit that I do like to bring a trout to net, but I don't get too upset if a 16-incher gets loose before I net it. There has to be more than one 16-inch trout in a lifetime of fly fishing doesn't there? Maybe I'll land the next one.

Check your landing net, or the one you plan to purchase, to determine what the bag is made of. A soft cotton mesh is the best. They're becoming difficult to find these days, but they're still available. Hard plastic netting and some nylon bags can damage the fish's protective slimy covering, and may be abrasive to its skin. Carry a soft cotton glove with you and put it on if you're handling the fish for a prolonged time while you're reviving it. You can get a much better grip with a gloved hand if you grab the fish just in front of the tail as you hold its head into the current. A firm grip won't do any damage to the fish's internal organs and is a good way to hold the fish for the hero shot when you get a big one. They aren't so apt to slip away at exactly the wrong moment.

One of my favorite ways of removing the fly is to slide my forefinger down the tippet in such a way that my fingernail will come in contact with the hook bend or the hook eye. Then I push backwards and the fly slides out of its hold.

Toss the fly and tippet to one side, turn the trout right side up, and hold its nose into a slowly moving current. You can do this while the trout

Fly fisher reviving a large trout.

is still in your net by guiding its nose into the current with your left hand. Allow your net frame to drift back until it's just under the fish's chin. The fish will swim away when it's ready. Watch it for a few minutes. Sometimes it will swim away for two or three feet until it can get behind something and go belly up. It's a dead fish if you don't get it back into your net right side up and spend some more time reviving it. Take it to one side where the current is slack and hold it by its tail as you cradle its chin in your other hand. Face it into the current and slowly and rhythmically push it back and forth in the current. This may take a few minutes if the fight was a long one, and the fish was whipped when you landed it. When the fish is ready, it will make its burst toward freedom with a quick swish of its tail. That's a good feeling. But watch it, just to make sure it's OK.

It's relatively easy to release small fish of 10 or 11 inches without netting them or picking them up out of the water. It usually doesn't take very long to land fish of this size, so it probably won't be necessary to worry much about reviving them. I do watch them swim away just to be certain they're in good shape. Never just drop them back in the stream, no matter how small they are. They're all treasures and should be treated as such.

One last tip about releasing your catch: Watch your trout swim away not only to make sure that it's recovered but also to see where it goes. It will immediately head for some cover or safe holding spot. I can't begin to tell you how many times a trout has shown me a holding spot that I had overlooked. Oftentimes this is merely a little depression in the stream bottom that's not apparent to a casual glance.

10

Float Fishing

If you get a chance to do some float fishing, take it. It's another way of adding challenge and excitement to an already exciting sport. Before you go, there are some things you need to do and understand if you want to have a pleasurable experience.

When you're float fishing, you'll need some information and some equipment that's not necessary when you walk and wade. First you need to know the name of the stream; how big it is; what lives in it; what kind of craft you will be in; how many hours you will be on the water; the name of the guide (boatman); his or her experience; what the guide provides in the way of flies, lunch, and drinks; and how many people will be in your boat.

Call the guide and find out what hatches might be present, what fish species are prevalent, and what tackle is recommended. Don't ask, "What's the lightest rod I can take?" Remember that your guide is an expert on this river and could probably catch 4-pounders on a 3-weight 7-foot rod. You are the newby here, and you should go armed for big game. I strongly suggest a 6-weight rod at least 8½ feet long that will throw a WF 7 F line with authority. This length rod will help you keep your backcast over the head of your guide and anyone else in the boat. There is nothing more embarrassing than hooking your guide with a sloppy backcast. If it happens once, you'll probably be forgiven. You'll no doubt be cursed if it happens a second time, and you better know how to swim if it happens a third time! Lighter weight rods are fun, but you'll probably need the muscle that a heavier rod can provide.

Do ask if there is space in the boat for you to bring a backup rod, and by all means, leave it in its case. A spare rod that's strung up in a float boat has a 99 percent chance of getting broken.

Many of your casts will be no more than twenty to thirty feet in length. A WF 7 line will load a 6-weight rod sooner and therefore require very little false casting. Most of your casting will be of the pick-up-and-lay-down variety as the boat goes downstream at what seems breakneck speed. Each cast is a one-shot effort, so it has to be presented exactly where you're looking. The ability to cast your fly into a teacup at twenty-five feet is the kind of accuracy you need. You simply won't have many opportunities to make a couple of backcasts to lengthen line because, by the time you do all that, you've already passed the target area. Keep some small loops of line in your line hand in case you suddenly need to lengthen your cast.

If you and your buddy are going to make the float trip with a guide, come to a clear agreement about how you're going to rotate front and rear positions in the boat. The guide may have some recommendations about this. The person in the front of the boat has a distinct advantage in that he can present his fly more times to a greater expanse of water than the person in the rear of the boat. This is especially true for right-handers when you're floating down the left side of the stream. The person in the rear of the boat is responsible for watching the person in the front. The person in the rear must time his pickups and forward casts to alternate with the person in front, or you'll end up with constant tangles from crossing backcasts. That is to say, the person in the rear must wait until the person in the front presents his fly before picking up his line to make another cast. Sometimes fishers will change positions after the front man catches a fish. Another option is to put time a limit on the front position, switching every hour.

The person in the front of the boat needs to be considerate of the person in the back. Think of the front of the boat as 12:00. Never allow your fly to drift below a 9:00 or 3:00 position from the front of the boat. If you are in front, you can lay out a cast well ahead of the boat and get very long drag-free floats that present the fly in front of the leader. Since the boat usually travels a little faster than the current, you'll be able to achieve thirty- to forty-foot drag-free floats over prime unfished water. Once your fly reaches the 9:00 or 3:00 position from the boat, you are fishing your

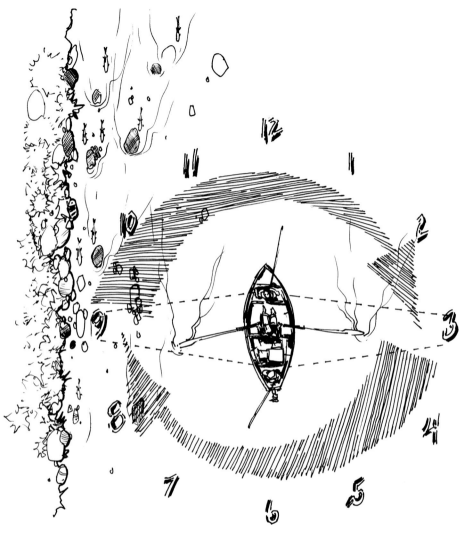

Two fly fishers in a Mac boat with guide in the center. The clock dial shows the area that each fisher can comfortably fish without infringing on his partner's water.

buddy's water. The person in the back normally can only cast up to the 10:00 or 2:00 position and allow his fly to trail to no more than a 7:00 or 5:00 position. It's bad form to hook a nice trout when your fly is at a 4:00 or 8:00 position, right in front of your buddy who is all set to cast to the same fish. It's probably going to happen once or twice during a daylong trip, but if it happens more than that, the front person is a fish hog.

Remember to keep your rod horizontal with the tip pointed well away from your partner when you're not actually fishing! Never lay your rod down in such a way that the tip section is behind or in front of your buddy. Not only will that probably screw up a cast for him, but you could end up with a broken tip. Immediately flip your fly and line to the other side of the boat and reel in when your partner hooks up with a fish. It's not uncommon for pandemonium to set in when your partner is fighting a fish, the boat is careening downstream, the guide is reaching for the net with one hand while trying to keep the boat aligned with the other hand on an oar, and you are trying to see what's going on. It's the very moment when accidents happen. Stay seated and hold onto your rod. You'll get to see the fish after it's netted, and the guide won't have to worry about you falling overboard. Both the guide and the person fighting the fish will be changing positions frequently, and the boat balance is constantly changing. If you're seated, the guide can keep his eye on the fish fighter and concentrate on maintaining the balance. I'll repeat: Stay seated and hold onto your rod. Get your camera ready in case it's a big one.

The guide and both fly fishers in the boat should give bank or wade fishers all the space they can. Never cast in front of them. And for heaven's sake make sure your backcast doesn't even come close to them. It's best to skip over about twenty or thirty yards of stream when you approach other anglers who are earthbound. Let your guide decide what to do when approaching another boat. My preference is to wait for them to get well downstream. Float fishermen do not spook the trout for very long simply because they aren't in front of the fish for more than a few seconds. I have a little problem with racing around another boat just to get in front of them. Wave at them, say, "Hi, how ya doin'?" and try to be friendly. It's far better to have friends on the water than enemies. Besides, they may offer some tips on what they've been having luck with.

For floating, you don't need waders that come up to your armpits. Waist-high waders are ideal when making a float trip. Your upper body stays cool, and you can reach into your shirt pockets. Hip boots are nice, but I've yet to make a float trip wearing hippers when I didn't scoop a gallon of water down one leg when I bailed back into the boat. You'll need waders when the boat is beached, and you can do some walk and wade fishing in remote areas. But check with your guide. You may not need waders or hippers if you're not getting out of the boat until the float is over.

I don't advise wearing a fully loaded vest. My favorite tackle bag is a daypack. It'll hold more fly boxes than you'll need (the guide will have plenty, but you'll probably be charged for those you use), a rain shell, an extra fleece garment, a canteen of water, sunscreen, bug repellent, a small multitool, extra tippet, and floatant, and you can pin a clipper or scissors to your shirt. There's usually a compartment where you can stow the day-pack while you're fishing. Don't leave your pack or bag lying around in the bottom of the boat. All those little straps and buckles will grab a loose loop of fly line every chance they get. If you fall overboard wearing a fully loaded vest, you'll probably go to the bottom like a rock. That could be a complication.

Do you tip the guide? Yes. I've done it a number of ways. I once tipped a guide way too much simply because it was a day that I caught way more fish than I deserved, he was a very pleasant companion to spend a day with, and didn't scream *"strike"* when a fish ate my fly. I once did not tip a guide just because he did scream *"strike"* every time a fish ate my fly, even after I asked him not to and further indicated that I could actually see the strikes myself. Every time he screamed *"strike"* I broke off my fly by setting up way too hard. I've been told that tipping a guide should be based on 10 to 20 percent of the fee, much like tipping a waiter or waitress at a restaurant. It depends on the quality of service you think you received. The tip shouldn't be based on how many fish you caught or how large they were. The guide can only take you to places where he or she knows there are fish. It's up to you to listen carefully to what the guide tells you, and then do what you're told. The guide can't put the fish on the hook or make them eat your fly. Weather conditions, water conditions, fish moods, hatch activity, your karma for the day, all play a role in what kind of day you'll have. None of which has anything to do with the guide.

Finally, invite your guide to fish. Most won't, but if he or she does, watch carefully. You can count on learning something.

11

Is That All There Is?

The winter of 2002 seemed to last forever. It was too cold most days to venture out with a fly rod. On those days when it might have been bearable to stand in ice cold water up to my knees, there was always some pressing matter, like tying an order of flies, that needed my immediate attention.

That winter in Colorado we had very little snow. By the middle of May there was so little water in many of our streams that the fisheries people were worried that many of the trout would not survive in streams that were already flowing at less than 25 percent of the normal August levels. It wasn't until the end of the month, May 23, that we finally had the first measurable precipitation since the previous September.

My mind tends to wander during the tying jobs, thinking about what might happen to the trout, will the bugs survive, remembering fishing a particular fly on a certain stream, how the day went, a difficult trout, and how the stream has changed over the years. I begin thinking of questions I'd like to ask someone, anyone. I want to find some answers and try to figure out who might have them. And then I wonder what I would do with the answers once I found them.

I've been at this fly-fishing thing for enough years that I'm now to the point where one question keeps popping into my head with increasing frequency: Where in the hell is fly fishing headed?

There was a time when fiberglass rods were all the rage. Then graphite took over our minds and the market. Lighter and shorter rods were supposed to provide us with thrills we only dreamed about before their invention. A few years later, we were told we should be fishing lighter lines on longer rods, and that idea evolved down to the 0-weight rod. That really bothered my logical mind because I figured if a 1-weight rod weighs something, then a 0-weight must weigh nothing. I toyed around with the idea of writing a piece about a –1-weight rod. A person could plug it into a computer and go fly-fishing virtually anyplace! I'm glad no one invented the ½-weight rod. It wouldn't be too slow or too fast, and soon would be known as the . . . well, you know where I'm headed with that one.

Now spey rods are all the rage. People will look at you as if you are really a dunce if you don't own at least one 14-foot two-handed rod. I learned to fish as a kid with a 14-foot bamboo pole. I was so small it took both hands to hold it. The chalk string on it was about the same diameter as the fly lines used on spey rods. My first experience at fly fishing was when my dad and I would impale a live grasshopper on a bait hook and roll-cast it out onto the stream with our bamboo poles. It vaguely resembled a spey cast. Maybe my idea of the –1-weight rod isn't such a bad idea. It's the logical next step. How did we catch all those fish before the latest new product came along?

But getting back to the question that keeps me up at night. Where will fly fishing be for your children and grandchildren? If you don't have any children, who is going to pass the torch you were handed? Who taught you stream ethics? Barbless hooks? Catch-and-release? Resting a pool? Sharing a pool?

Who's teaching the love of the sport these days? Whose responsibility is it? Is it something that can be taught or are certain blessed souls born with it? Is it merely a love of fly fishing or awe and respect for nature and all its marvels? Does a newcomer need a mentor to drop little gems of wisdom? Little seeds of thought? Like how to wade silently or avoid stepping on wildflowers or redds, how to give the other guy his space. How to walk well away from the streamside when passing a fellow angler. How to lovingly land and release a fine trout. What is a fine trout?

Can a new fly fisher enjoy catching only one trout in a day of fishing? Can an experienced fly fisher? Should you? How can you? Should you quit fishing when your first fish of the day is the largest fish of your life and it's 9:00 A.M.? How many fish per day do you need to land to call it a successful day? Do numbers of fish per day really count for something? What? At what number do you lose count of the fish you've caught? Do we need to catch "enough fish" to begin thinking about this? How many is enough? How much do you enjoy watching your fishing partner catch more fish than you? Are our actions governed by some primordial instinct to capture, dominate, or prove manhood? Is that really a viable thought today? Why do the tackle manufacturers use only photos with big fish? Or why do SUV manufacturers show video clips of their powerful four-wheel-drive vehicles grinding through foot-deep, crystal clear mountain streams with macho voice-overs? Don't women drive SUVs?

Is it the manufacturers' responsibility to be concerned about all the above? Are they doing enough to educate the public to respect their fellow fly fishers as well as what nature *currently* provides? If it isn't their duty, whose is it? Should the responsibility be shared with retailers and their customers? Should fly-fishing magazines and their writers spend more time and space on these questions? Would anyone read it if they did? What about Trout Unlimited and the Federation of Fly Fishers or state fish and game management agencies? Have they done all they can? Are they merely taking care of today's needs or tomorrow's? What more can they do? Are we doing enough?

Anyone can find detailed instructions on where to go, which guide to hire, what tackle to use, what clothes to pack, which boat to buy, which motels and restaurants are highly recommended, which flies to tie, best times to go, tidal charts, stream flows, which line shoots best, and on and on and on. Oftentimes these recommendations are accompanied with scientifically documented charts and graphs. I'd guess about 98 percent of the information available on fly fishing has only to do with catching fish. Catching fish *is* the main goal, but that can't be all there is to fly fishing. And that thought brings yet more questions.

What does it matter if conservation groups and some manufacturers buy up or lease land and water rights and make them public, if the public doesn't respect the resource or the ownership? If you owned two hundred acres with a spring-fed stream on it, would you allow others to fish it? How do we get those who don't care to begin caring? Do those who say they care really care enough? Are the purchases and leases governed to any degree by advertising, memberships, or future sales? If you had a spare two or three hundred dollars, would you join a private fishing lease?

What is your ultimate goal when you fish your home water? Why do you think that? What is your ultimate goal when you travel to some fabled waters to fish? Why do you think that? Is there a difference? Should there be?

Does one need to fish alone to begin to find some of the answers to the above questions? Have you ever stopped fishing during a hatch with rising trout to sit a while to consider the wonder of it?

Can a person with a 50-year-old J.C. Higgins fiberglass rod and an old Pflueger reel enjoy a day on the stream as much as the person fifty yards downstream with equipment that's worth $1,200 or $1,500? I'd like to think there is some kind of connection or bond between the two, because at the end of the day each fly fisher will clip off a $1.85 fly and save it! If there is a connection, is that where we begin to look for answers?

Do we all need to get out in the woods (lost maybe?) to begin to understand that there is a difference between man's rules and nature's? Do you pick up a two-foot length of tippet, cigarette butt, plastic wrapper, or beverage can someone else left behind? Ever leave one? If you toss a length of tippet into the grass, how many people will see it? Would you like them all to know it was you who tossed it? How many people do you think will walk by before it's picked up? Do you care? Can one person make a difference? When you kill a fish to take home for the occasional meal of fresh fish, do you get more pleasure from the food or showing it to your friends and neighbors?

I once fished with a man who had just returned from Alaska, where he had caught hundreds of huge salmon, char, and steelhead. There was still a gleam in his eye as he told me about it while we were stringing up our rods to fish a small Colorado mountain stream. We decided to leapfrog the pools and stay together as we worked our way upstream. I was soon sorry I had come with him because every time he landed an 8- or 10-inch trout, he tossed it back into the water from waist high as if, because they were small fish, it didn't matter how they were treated. Is that all there is to trout fishing? I never fished with him again.

When you fish a lot, you invariably fish in many different places near and far from home. I've fished in enough near and far places now to begin spending a little more time looking. Not so much at the water, but at what is near it. I learn a little about where the stream is born and how it grows as it reaches its ultimate end. Which in a way is similar to my own life. I don't much like anyone messing around with either one.

I fished in Labrador over July 4, 2001. While there, I fished a stream that to anyone's knowledge before my visit had never had a fly cast on it. It's a sobering experience. Ancient logs were covered with a thick carpet of lush green moss. Foot-deep caribou moss covered every inch of ground, and I had to be careful not to stumble over it. No fishermen's or hiking trails; just caribou trails that had been in use for centuries by countless herds. It would be a good place to meet one's maker.

As I approached the streambank, I stopped and thought that this must be what much of the continental United States looked like before we arrived. Unspoiled, unchanged, unimproved, untrespassed, unfenced, pure raw wilderness. The stream was crystal clear, and I could see huge wild brook trout, pike, and whitefish finning in their holding places. It was a scene as pristine as a Disney movie studio could produce. Only this was all so true that even the most imaginative artist couldn't come close to creating the perfection of it.

As I made my first cast and watched the size 8 Royal Wulff float jauntily along a current crease, I realized I was probably the first white man to fish these waters. And I was interrupting the delicate balance that was so evident everywhere I looked. I thought about all the streams in the United States that aren't wild like this one, streams lined with cabins, boat docks, groomed lawns, enhanced holding pools, carports, fire pits made of brick and steel, leveled and graveled campsites, RV parks with twenty-foot spaces, and plastic picnic tables with signs that say "Don't Feed The Bears." I thought of how much of our good earth we've turned into paved parking lots, how we've worn down our hiking and fishing trails and put up signs that warn "No Parking," "No Overnight Camping," "No Fires," "Stay On The Trail," "Have A Nice Day, Enjoy Your Wilderness." And what comes to mind is the Jerry Leiber/Mike Stoller song made famous by Peggy Lee, "Is That All There Is?"

I play and land the huge brook trout that has eaten my fly on the first cast. I release it with a burst of laughter and some tears and secretly hope that no one will ever find this place. I'm both grateful to have found it and sorry that I intruded. And I smile because suddenly I realize I have found the answer to Peggy Lee's question. This is all there is, and we all damn sure better begin to do more to keep what remains before another song is written whose title is: "Is This All That's Left?"

I have fished with some guides who make every effort to protect the resource, almost to the point of covering our footprints in the caribou moss. It's heartwarming to watch that kind of tender care. On the other end of the scale, I have heard of a guide who stands on the top of his vehicle with a hailer directing as many as five clients at a time on where to stand and where to cast.

Maybe fly fishing today has more to do with expectations than it did some years ago. Fly fishers expect to catch more fish when they buy new and expensive equipment. The shop or lodge owner who is advertising magnificent fishing expects return customers and repeat sales. The guides expect to keep their jobs and receive tips, so they do nearly anything they can to put clients into fish. The manufacturers produce equipment that they expect consumers will purchase in order to be more successful when they hire guides or go to their favorite streams. And the fly fisher goes to the stream expecting to catch 22-inch trout that weigh 6 pounds and more, the ones they have seen in all the advertisements. I know; I'm one of them.

But where do we draw that thin wavy gray line between expectations and reality?

In spite of all the litter, rules, overuse, encroachment, high-tech equipment, glitzy ads, and ignorance, each spring brings new promise. The birds sing, and the swelling buds tell us, "It's not too late yet, I will help you if you will let me. I do have the answers if you don't expect too much."

Or as the song says, "If that's all there is my friend, then let's keep dancing, let's break out the booze and have a ball."

It's a short song.

Index